Bright Ideas
Environmental Studies

Written by Alistair Ross

Contents

Published by Scholastic Publications Ltd,
Marlborough House, Holly Walk,
Leamington Spa, Warwickshire CV32 4LS.

Written by Alistair Ross
Edited by Jane Bishop and Jackie
  Cunningham-Craig
Designed by Sue Limb
Illustrated by Fred Haycock

Printed in Great Britain by Loxley Brothers
Ltd, Sheffield

© 1988 Scholastic Publications Ltd
Reprinted in 1989

ISBN 0 590 70952 6

Front and back cover: photographs by
Martyn Chillmaid, designed by Sue Limb

Introduction

Environmental studies provide an opportunity for children to find out about the area around them – its people, its places, its past and how it works. Ideas in this book are divided into specific locations, such as at school or by the river, but they all form a range of activities designed for primary school children to find out about their world.

HOW TO USE THIS BOOK

This book is divided into a number of environmental themes. Often these overlap. Within each theme you will find listed a number of bright ideas: each tells what age range is most appropriate. Some ideas are straightforward one-offs – they need little in the way of preparation or follow-up. Others may need much more in the way of preparation, and should be seen as stimulating your ideas about what to do next month or next term, rather than tomorrow!

Finally, these are only generalised ideas. Your environment is unique to you and your children. How you help them explore it will naturally depend very much on your local conditions.

ABOUT THE SCHOOL

Although the environment is 'out there', it doesn't stop at the school gates! Classrooms and schools also offer examples of a particular kind of environment, and this section looks at some unfamiliar environment uses that can be made from what is immediately to hand. However, just because they are so accessible, don't assume that these environmental issues are not well worth exploring.

DOWN THE STREET

The local street may sound rather too familiar to repay extended study, but there are hundreds of activities that a class can undertake within a few yards of the school. The activities in this chapter show what can be done in any street if you look with care at what is there.

SHOPS AND MARKETS

The local shops are part of almost all children's everyday experience. Before school, most children are taken into shops almost daily, and begin to acquire a whole range of ideas about exchange, money and value. This section offers some local starting points from shops that can be easily adapted to fit any locality.

CITY LIFE

Towns and cities are full of social and scientific material from which children can learn a great deal. The ideas in this chapter merely scratch at the surface of this rich resource.

RIVER AND SEA

Not all schools are close to the sea, or to rivers that allow much in the way of a close environmental study. But, within the space of the school year, classes often visit areas where some of these activities will be possible. Special care should be taken with safety near water – a moment's inattention or lack of organisation in or around water can have fatal results. Make sure that as many as possible of your pupils have learned to swim.

Before visiting a water site with pupils, check for specific features of the site such as tide times, unstable banks etc. Never allow pupils to indulge in informal paddling or swimming in unknown waters. Always bear the weather conditions (both current and forecast) in mind.

VILLAGE AND COUNTRY

The countryside offers as rich a learning environment as the town. This chapter, though it focuses on an area that may be remote for most of our urban-based schools, offers suggestions that may be of use during school visits, residential journeys and the like, as well as to country schools.

AROUND THE YEAR

The environment changes over the year, and some activities are more suitable in particular months, or may only be possible in certain seasons. This section also includes ways of investigating changes in the weather.

AWAY FROM SCHOOL

If you are planning to leave school, organisation and awareness of potential dangers will obviously ensure smooth running of the activities planned. Whether you are simply crossing the road to carry out your traffic census or actually going out on a trip, important safety issues arise.

Check what regulations your LEA has made for the number of teachers and/or adults who must accompany a party of children out of school. This will vary according to the number and age of the children concerned.

Always remember that no child under seven years of age (and many who are older!) should be expected or allowed to cross a road unaided. Their lack of perception of speed and distance make this unsafe. It is important that adequate supervision is always provided even for the simplest road-crossing task.

If you are going out on a school trip, pre-planning will obviously include booking in advance, toilet and refreshment provision, as well as contingency plans for illness and clearing up rubbish. For safety's sake make sure that all children know what to do if they get separated from their group or supervisor. Remember that when you are caring for children away from school your responsibility to them is as though you were their parent.

RESOURCES

The Royal Society for the Prevention of Accidents (RoSPA), Cannon House, Priory Queensway, Birmingham B4 6BS, tel 021 200 2461, produces a range of literature including posters, leaflets, filmstrips and videos on all aspects of pupil safety. Write to the Safety Education Department at the above address for a full catalogue of materials.

Starting out

The local environment

The environment isn't an area of the curriculum that is solely based on books, television programmes, project packs or posters, although these are invaluable back-up resources. The starting point for nearly all the projects suggested in this book is the social and physical surroundings of the child.

Environmental studies offers a broad way to approach a group of different elements in the curriculum. It includes, for example, scientific processes to explain environmental phenomena, such as the weather and the flora and fauna of a locality. A group of geographical skills are developed in exploring the spatial relationships of people, their activities, and natural events and things.

There is often a need to explore along a historical dimension to discover – or to hypothesise – about how an environmental feature developed. And there is the social environment to consider; for example, how have people used, changed, and been affected by their surroundings?

From infancy, children have been experiencing and responding to their environment, and have tried to build up explanations for how their world works. We can build on these experiences and explanations in primary school, and the activities in this book will offer ideas targetted at specific ages, although teachers will be able to adapt and use most of the ideas for any age range.

Processes

Children in primary school have a natural desire to catalogue and classify their observations of the world about them. It is part of the way that they come to conclusions about how their environment works and affects them. Adults too generalise about their surroundings, but we are building on processes and experiences that began in childhood.

The process is essentially a spiral: we observe something going on; we attempt to build a rule from this; we make more observations; we modify our rule to fit in the new data; we make more observations; we modify; and so on.

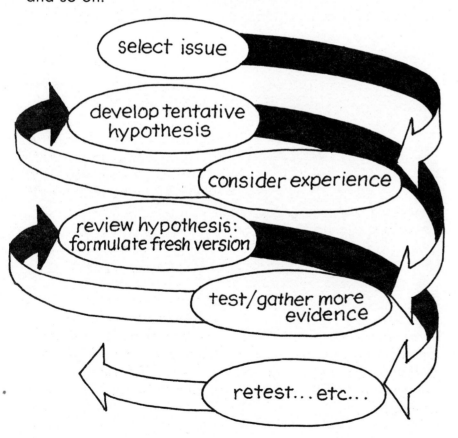

select issue

develop tentative hypothesis

consider experience

review hypothesis: formulate fresh version

test/gather more evidence

retest... etc...

Skills

There is a whole variety of skill learning going on during good environmental work. Much of this is in the area of the traditional 'basic' skills, where the environmental focus does more than just reinforce skills of literacy and numeracy, but often provides some very real purpose for getting these skills right.

There are skills of careful observation including looking with precision, searching for detail, monitoring change, and measuring data. These skills may involve careful drawing from life, using measuring devices, or even a camera or tape recorder.

Skills of observation need to be followed with

8

evaluative skills. What does what has been seen mean? What are the implications? Why did it happen?

Both observations and conclusions need to be communicated, and there are more skills to be used here. Choosing the most effective method, whether it is drawing, writing, a diagram or a play, is in itself a skill.

The ability to use charts, diagrams, tables and maps to communicate ideas is becoming increasingly important. It is now vital to be able to select relevant facts and data from the great abundance of information that surrounds us, and to be able to demonstrate just why these particular facts are important. The microcomputer is beginning to help us develop this skill, so that children learn how to select and create their own graphical explanations of their surroundings, as well as interpreting other people's graphical data.

Much environmental study also involves children working together collaboratively, and these activities develop a range of social and co-operative skills that are of value. Sharing ideas and talents is often an undervalued skill, and by no means an easy one to develop.

Concepts

It often helps the teacher to have a mental check-list of key ideas to develop in an area such as environmental studies. Concepts are simple ideas, expressed in a shorthand word or group of words, which can be used to sort and classify our ideas. The following list is not supposed to be definitive.

- Authority: the ability to take charge, based on one's position or particular capabilities.
- Cause and effect: the linking together of what might be necessary and/or sufficient conditions so that particular consequences follow.
- Change: in physical properties; in a life cycle; through economic, social, political or technological causes.
- Co-operation: working together to solve a problem or complete a task more easily than working alone.
- Conflict: in any environment, physical or social, there will be competition for scarce resources.
- Division of labour: work is divided into separate parts to make the job more efficient, easier or cheaper.
- Experiment: a way of trying to prove the truth or falsity of a statement.
- Interdependence: the way that people, plants, or animals depend on others to do certain things for them.
- Power: the ability to make others do what one wants, or the capacity to use energy.
- Representation: using signs and symbols to convey meaning, as on a map; or where a person acts on behalf of a group, for example, in a council.
- Sequence: the order in which events happen.
- Scale: using proportional signs or symbols to convey information about distance and size.
- Social control: making and enforcing social rules or laws which make people conform to expectations and conventions.

- Test: a fair way of examining some event, often repeated to see if it holds over several instances, and to find out the limits of a prediction or hypothesis.
- Tradition: customary ways of doing things, ideas and habits about everyday events.

Concepts are not formulae or definitions to be learned and repeated. They are slowly built up and extended by repeatedly meeting examples, by comparing them with experience of other examples, and by sharing ideas with others through discussion.

Attitudes and knowledge

Studying the environment should lead to children developing important attitudes towards their surroundings, their community and themselves, and towards learning. These attitudes should include a sense of caring for the environment, and to appreciate its complexity, as well as sensitivity for the ways in which different communities operate. A willingness to examine evidence and experience, and to discuss and debate ideas with others, should also be encouraged.

There's a wealth of factual information about the environment, but it is important not to let this get out of perspective. Knowledge in itself is not very useful unless the children learn how to apply it to particular situations, how to find more information when they need it, and how to assess it critically.

This way of using knowledge is not easy to develop, but is a crucial task for the teacher. It means encouraging children to take a cautious and tentative attitude to what they discover.

In and out of the classroom

Not all environmental studies can take place 'out there': much of it depends on getting initial data and stimuli from the surroundings, and capturing this in some way to bring back to the classroom. There it can be worked on later, at ease, and with the resources of the classroom, but it is important to keep returning to the environmental aspect being studied.

The field trip shouldn't be a one-off day out at the beginning of the study (still less should it come at the end of a study!). The visit to the environment, be it street, meadow, sea-shore, market or workplace, should provide some essential early input to a project, but should also be repeatedly revisited to answer questions that will arise. It is often the later questions in an environmental project that are the most probing.

About the school

Parents at school

Age range
Five to seven.

Group size
Small group to whole class.

What you need
A mum or dad, or several parents.

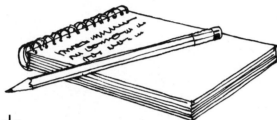

What to do
Ask the children to try to imagine whether their parents went to school and, if so, what school may have been like then. Accept without comment whatever ideas are put forward – even the more bizarre suggestions of dinosaur steaks for school dinners. If you can note down who said what, this may help children later to recall what they said. Next, suggest that the class find out what schools were really like when their parents were children. How can they find out?

Introduce a parent to the class and let the children test out their ideas about schooling then. It usually helps if you ask the parent to stick to their primary school education, rather than secondary school memories.

If there are several groups talking to different parents, ask the groups afterwards to tell each other what they have discovered. Use your list of the initial discussion to keep reminding them how their ideas have begun to change.

Follow-up
Try to find someone who attended your school 20 years ago, and get them to talk about how the buildings and classrooms have changed.

Get parents who were educated in different countries to talk about how their school system differed.

Classroom models

Age range
Five to seven.

Group size
Small groups.

What you need
Corrugated cardboard boxes, wallpaper scraps, adhesive, card, scissors, paint, modelling clay.

What to do
Each group cuts the front and top off a cardboard box, and makes a model of the classroom inside it. Encourage them to look as carefully as possible around the room, as often as they need. They will soon come up against problems of proportion and scale.

Keeping the box standing the same way as the classroom itself may help with proportion, and you can assist by helping them to cut windows and doors in the correct places so that they can keep their bearings.

Modelling clay figurines may help get the scale of the furniture right.

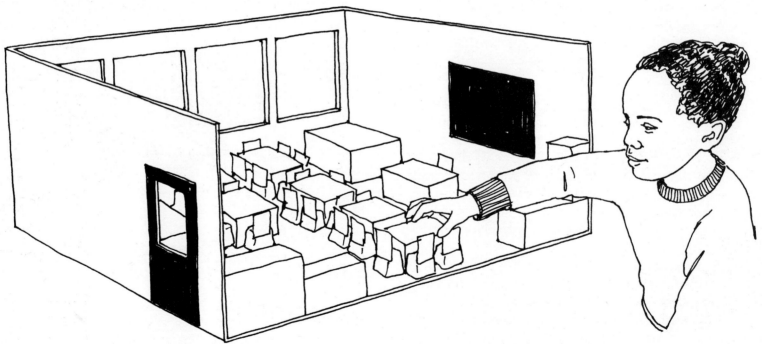

Follow-up
Build similar models of other classrooms (if your colleagues are sufficiently patient), and then assemble a school.

If the children have talked to an adult who was taught in the same classroom, they might try to make a model of it, based on the description given.

Visitors

Age range
Five to seven.

Group size
Small group to whole class.

What you need
Any adult who enters the class during one week.

What to do
Ask the children about who helps the school run well. Who are all the people they rely upon to help them? Make a list of them and get individual children to paint pictures of each person to illustrate the list.

  Then suggest that they count up who actually comes into the class, and find out exactly how they help. Question each person who comes into the classroom, either at the time or perhaps a little later if this is more convenient. Ask the children to compare what they thought the person did with what they actually do.

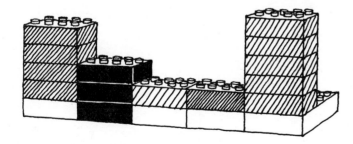

Follow-up
Use Lego building bricks to build a tally to check who comes in most often.

Milkman   5
Mrs Jones   2
Secretary   4

Picture clocks

Age range
Five to seven.

Group size
Small groups.

What you need
Card circles, card, paper-fasteners, pencils, crayons.

What to do
Ask children about when things happen in the school day. How long do they last?

Fasten the circle to the card background with a paper-fastener through the centre, as shown in Figure 1. Get the children to draw segments that show the sequence of activities through the day, using a picture and a word or two to show assembly, lessons, play, lunch etc.

Mark an arrow on the background card, and rotate the circle to show each activity in turn.

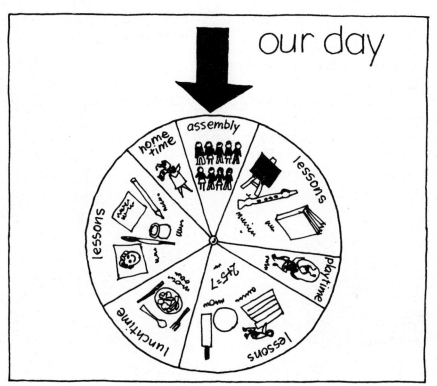

Figure 1

Gran's schooldays

Age range
Seven to nine.

Group size
Small or large groups.

What you need
Some willing grandparents, or similarly aged people.

What to do
Brief the grandparents: they will be asked about their life at school, and should try to stick to this as much as possible. Many grandparents will remember the wartime evacuation of school and rationing: both of these are events well worth concentrating upon.

Stress that it is more useful if they talk about what actually happened to them, rather than trying to explain the general war situation. This is partly because they know far more about these experiences (and can illustrate them with anecdotes), and partly because children will be able to empathise with stories of childhood.

Follow-up
Try to find other people evacuated from the same school, and talk with them. Find pictures of the local area in the war. You might even visit the place the children were evacuated to, and see if you can find any of their hosts.

Class litter count

Age range
Seven to nine.

Group size
Small groups and whole class.

What you need
The classroom towards the end of the day, educational supplies catalogue, calculator.

What to do
This activity is particularly useful when you are trying to encourage children to keep their classroom tidy. About half an hour before the end of the day, explain to the children that when they tidy up they are going to collect together everything they pick up. You could ask them to estimate how much they think there will be, and how much is wasted in the school each year. Then get them to make a really thorough search behind cupboards and bookcases, and so on.

Pile everything up and then get a group to start sorting it out, and another to compile a list. As the pile mounts up, the children will probably enter into the spirit of the exercise and redouble their efforts to keep the classroom tidy in future. Tell the children that it isn't the cleaner's job to pick everything up and sort it out.

Next day, using an educational supplies catalogue, get a group to cost the value of everything that was found. They may need a calculator for this, especially when it comes to items like 17 sheets of paper.

Finally, add the groups' totals together and find the average. If there is £1.15 worth of materials wasted in one day, for example, how much is used in a week, a school year and for the whole school?

Follow-up
This activity ought to result in a tidier environment! Follow it up with a similar exercise a couple of weeks later. Compare the results.

Of course, sometimes the activity isn't entirely fair. If one pair of scissors lost behind a cupboard gets multiplied by 180 school days, and by the number of classes in the school, the bill immediately runs into thousands of pounds.

The milk round

Age range
Seven to nine.

Group size
Groups and whole class.

What you need
A friendly milk deliverer.

What to do
Waylay the school milk delivery person, and ask if he or she would be prepared to talk with the class about their job. Offer to write to the depot manager for permission (dairies are usually quite keen on this sort of public relations work).

Briefly explain that you would like them to talk about their part in the process of getting milk from the farm to the consumer, and for the children to ask about the work.

It is probably best to have the talk with the whole class, and then for the milk delivery person to circulate to three or four groups for questions. The class may also be able to look at the milk-float.

Encourage the class to look at the pros and cons of the hours of work, the need for reliability, and the interdependence of all the people working in the milk delivery system.

Follow-up
Have a full-scale study of milk production, which might involve a visit to a farm (several specialise in milking a few cows during school hours, especially for visiting parties), or a milk-bottling plant.

A survey of children's home life to see what kinds of milk are drunk, such as full, semi-skimmed, skimmed etc, could produce some interesting results.

Minibeasts around the school

Age range
Seven to nine.

Group size
Small groups.

What you need
Pooters, animal identification keys, empty jars, scraps of food.

What to do
Groups try to find as many different kinds of animals around the school as possible. Make insect traps from jars with fairly small holes in the lid, to prevent some species from getting trapped in them, and put a little food into each jar. Try bread, a few drops of honey, grains of sugar etc.

Leave the jars in various corners, behind cupboards, and in different rooms. You will need to alert the school caretaker and the cleaners first.

Check the traps each morning, and get the children to classify what they collect. They should also note where particular minibeasts are found, and what foods attract them. Likely animals are ants, silverfish, cockroaches, and flies. Make sure all insects are returned to their natural habitat afterwards.

Follow-up
A search through some reference books on the life styles of some of these minibeasts will show how unhygienic they are, and why their presence in school is undesirable.

Extend the survey into the playground, setting traps at the end of the school day and collecting them just before school starts.

Unravelling the past

Age range
Nine to eleven.

Group size
Pairs or small groups.

What you need
Nothing specific.

What to do
Most schools are continually being modified by minor building changes – an electric point is added here, a new heating system there, new paint, more plumbing etc. In most schools, these are piled up one over the other, and the order in which things happened can be worked out by looking at how the various systems overlap.

For example, a classroom wall may have this arrangement of services.

From this one can deduce that the original lighting system was installed first, and then (perhaps at the same time) the cold water system. This was probably followed by hot water, then a gas pipe, and finally a new electric light circuit.

Children can trace these clues and others, such as the colours beneath chipped paintwork, changes in brickwork patterns and so on, to reconstruct the sequence of how their classroom has changed. It calls for quite close observation, and perhaps some help from the school caretaker in identifying the various types of pipes.

Follow-up
The education department or the local library may have old photographs of your school classroom. These can supplement this work, and children can start to match dates to some of the changes.

Extend the idea to other rooms in the school, or to other buildings.

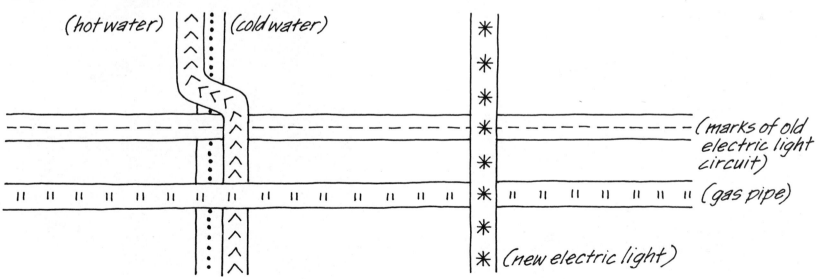

(hot water) (cold water) (marks of old electric light circuit) (gas pipe) (new electric light)

Litter around the school

Age range
Nine to eleven.

Group size
Pairs or small groups.

What you need
Polythene bags, scales, a dustbin liner, disposable polythene gloves (an optional extra), copies of page 117.

What to do
Each group is given a specific area of the public parts of the school (ie corridors or playgrounds rather than classrooms or the headteacher's office). One afternoon, get the children to undertake a really thorough tidy, putting all the rubbish in their area into their bags.

Get them to sort it out and classify it. What items are causing the litter problem in your school? Which are the areas that are worst affected? What can be done about it?

Follow-up
Launch an anti-litter campaign, with posters in strategic places. Monitor it: does it work?

Use the questionnaire on other classes about their opinions on litter.

Who works in our school?

Age range
Nine to eleven.

Group size
Groups or whole class.

What you need
Paper, paints and coloured pencils, adhesive, scissors.

What to do
With the help of the whole class, make a list of all the people who work in the school by writing down their names and jobs. Don't forget all the kitchen staff, the cleaners, helpers, and the school secretary. You may have a debate about whether to include people who work part-time, such as peripatetic teachers.

Each person is drawn and the pictures are coloured: try to agree on an approximate size before this starts. Then each is carefully cut out. They could be temporarily pinned in line, so that the whole group can be seen. Discuss ways of arranging them – what different systems of grouping could be used?

Then ask the children to arrange the pictures in a pattern to show how the school works. Who would go at the top? (If they say the school caretaker and secretary are really in charge of the school, just consider for a moment that they might be right!) After some discussion, an interesting hierarchy of the school will emerge.

Follow-up
Discuss if there are other ways in which the school could be organised. Is a hierarchy essential? Get a school governor to talk with the class about the constraints on the powers of the headteacher.

A teacher's day

Age range
Seven to eleven.

Group size
Small groups.

What you need
A patient colleague, paper and pencils.

What to do
What do teachers do all day? Get the group to talk amongst themselves, first about what they think teachers do. Then get them to talk to a colleague about what they do, including, of course, preparation, work at home, curriculum planning and INSET. The group might prepare a chart of the work done, or a pie chart of segments. This

activity is always followed by a great deal of sympathy by children towards teachers – they haven't the faintest idea how hard you work!

Follow-up
Other groups could interview other teachers, the headteacher, the school caretaker etc.

A temperature map

Age range
Nine to eleven.

Group size
Small groups.

What you need
Thermometers (at least one, but the more the better), squared paper.

What to do
Ask who feels warm and who feels cold. The answers will probably vary around the class. Then get groups to start to plot the temperatures around the room.

They could do this first by measuring the temperature in different parts of the room. They may need some help with the scales on the thermometer at first. One group can then make a scale map of the classroom on which temperatures can be written.

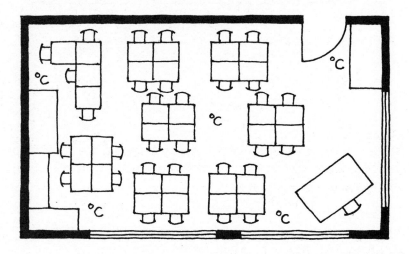

Someone may eventually point out that during the time all this takes, the temperature measured in the first place will probably have changed. Doors are opened, children move about, air currents move — all these variables can upset the temperature. The next stage is to keep a thermometer in the same place, and take a series of regular readings, at least every ten minutes. This can be plotted on a graph, with notes of anything likely to have caused a change eg 10.52: Martin opened the window.

Follow-up
Turn the map of classroom temperatures into a weather map by colouring in similar temperature squares the same colour, or drawing isotherms (lines showing the same temperature). Where are the cold spots? Does the temperature change over the day? What about different heights? Measure the temperature at floor level, and then as high as you can.

Design a playground

Age range
Seven to eleven.

Group size
Small groups.

What you need
Paper, pencils, coloured pens, modelling materials and paint (optional).

What to do
Ask the class what playgrounds are for. What sort of activities have to go on there, and what sort of things do different groups of children prefer to do?

Get them to list all the possibilities, and to think about what sort of space each activity needs.

Can they design an ideal playground? You could either encourage them to let their imagination run riot by using ponds, climbing frames, refreshment kiosks, or keep them strictly to the reality of redesigning your existing space.

Follow-up
Build a model of the area with equipment to scale.

Persuade the PTA to try to raise the funds to implement the most imaginative design!

Down the street

Old photographs

Age range
Five to eleven.

Group size
Small groups.

What you need
Copies of old photographs of your locality (a good source is your local council's archive department, which is usually part of the library services. They will have a collection of materials that you will almost certainly be able to copy for use in school), magnifying glasses, camera and film.

What to do
Select photographs of the local street taken at different times in the past. Get the children to try to identify where each shot was taken. If there are several from approximately the same viewpoint, they could try to decide the order in which they were taken. The magnifying glasses will help them to check for details.

Go out on the street and try to find the exact position and view. What are the differences? What features have remained the same?

Follow-up
Photograph the same view today. Date it and add it to the collection. Keep your photos – a teacher in the school ten years from now might find them very useful!

Street furniture

Age range
Five to eleven.

Group size
Small groups or the whole class.

What you need
Paper, pencils, clipboards. A camera may be useful.

What to do
Walk down the street, noting carefully all the different things that are found on the pavement and road. Don't miss obvious items, such as pillar-boxes and lamp-posts. There will also be service hatches for gas, water, phones etc, and Ordnance Survey marks, and lots more.

Back in school classify the features, find out more about them, and then get groups to survey the frequency and distribution of each on the street. Draw and photograph each type.

Follow-up
Does the adjacent street have the same kinds of street furniture?

House fronts

Age range
Five to nine.

Group size
Small groups or the whole class.

What you need
Paper, pencils, clipboards. A camera may be useful.

What to do
Walk down the street and get the children to look at house fronts in detail. Doors and windows can be particularly interesting. Look at the varieties of door panelling, the number of doorbells, and the types of windows. Many nineteenth-century terraces have elaborate mouldings around doorways and windows: are they identical?

Follow-up
Draw, photograph or make a model of what has been observed.

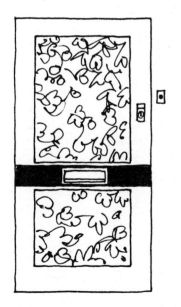

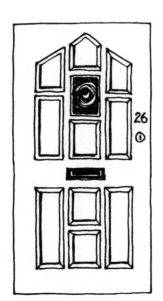

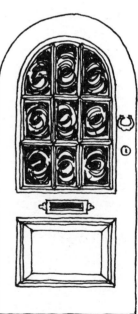

Old maps

Age range
Eight to eleven.

Group size
Small groups.

What you need
A series of maps of your locality, as detailed as possible (see 'What you need' on page 27 to find out where to obtain them.)

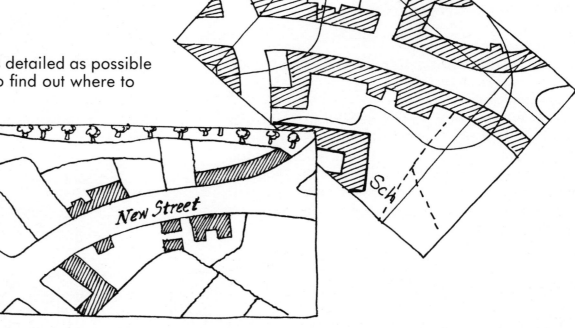

What to do
Select a small local street with which children are familiar. Trim all the maps that you use to cover the same area (you may want to enlarge fragments of maps – local photocopy shops can do this reasonably cheaply).

Use a modern map first, out in the street: help the children get familiar with the map and the features it shows. Back in class, get out the old maps and look for details of similarity and difference.

Ordnance Survey maps will be very detailed and give good comparisons. If you can find maps of the area before building took place, compare the shapes of the fields with the shapes of the roads. Builders often developed one field at a time, and the old field lines remain as the garden walls between rows of houses, or as roads.

Follow-up
Invent maps of in-between dates. Map the area as you imagine it will look in a hundred year's time.

Street directories

Age range
Nine to eleven.

Group size
Small groups or the whole class.

What you need
Copies of pages from old street directories. Choose the same street from each directory and, if there is a series of directories (one for each year), select every tenth or fifth year rather than one year at a time. (See 'What you need' on page 27 to find out where to obtain them.)

What to do
Street directories show who lived in each house and were the forerunner of telephone directories, but arranged geographically rather than by name.

You can usually work out which house each entry refers to by using contemporary maps. Get the children to plot the changes to each house, such as who lived in it and when. They can often plot a chronological sequence of a house's owners, and see the continuity as well as the changes.

36	38	40
Jones Broom	Brown	Smith

Junk terraces

Age range
Five to seven.

Group size
Small groups or pairs.

What you need
Corrugated card boxes, card, scissors, adhesive, paint.

What to do
Walk down the street and get each group or pair to select one house and study it carefully.

Back in class each pair takes a cardboard box, adds a roof, and paints the box to look like their house (they will probably have to guess what the back looks like!).

When they are all completed, get the children to assemble the boxes together to take up the shape of the street. A lot of valuable early mapping activities can develop from this.

Follow-up
If you have the space, stick the houses together. Add a base and paint the street. Add street furniture, people, and vehicles etc.

Street friezes

Age range
Seven to eleven.

Group size
Pairs or the whole class.

What you need
Paper, pencils, colouring pens and paints, scissors. It may also be helpful to have street directory extracts, copies of old maps and census returns for the same street. (See 'What you need' on page 27 to find out where these can be obtained.)

What to do
Each pair is allocated one house in the street (make sure you get a complete stretch of houses). They draw this carefully from life, making detailed notes on ornamentation, colours etc.

In class, decide on a common scale for the houses, and get each pair to draw and colour their house to scale. Then cut the houses out (write the numbers on the back first!) and stick them together as a frieze.

Underneath, add details from the census returns and street directories (and any other sources you have), showing who used to live in the house, and how it has changed over the years.

Follow-up
If you can work out which buildings have been re-built or radically changed, and when (use maps and photos), draw the original buildings to scale and have these on flaps that can be lowered over the frieze, to recreate the appearance of the street at different times.

Changing patterns

Age range
Nine to eleven.

Group size
Small groups.

What you need
Simple maps of the street, information from street directories etc.

What to do
Talk about the various types of uses that the buildings in the street were put to. Each building may have had a variety of roles, such as a shop, a factory and a home, or some classification of shop, such as a haberdasher's, throughout the years. Then decide on a colour key to represent these categories, and fill in a series of maps, one for each year about which you have information. Arrange the maps in sequence. Look for patterns of similarity and change of use.

Street workers

Age range
Seven to eleven.

Group size
Small groups.

What you need
Paper, pencils, clipboard. A tape recorder and a camera would be an advantage.

What to do
Who works in the street? This isn't directed at people who live or trade in it, but at people who actually do their work out-of-doors on the street, such as telephone engineers, postal workers, and newspaper deliverers.

Get the children to list all the different kinds of workers that they have seen on the street. A class discussion on the types of work would help: nearly everyone is concerned with bringing some kind of service to people who live on the street. Some repair regular (often underground) services; others deliver or sell goods to street users. Who do they work for, if anyone? How often do they work on that particular street? How well might they know the people who live there?

After hypothesising about these questions, small groups of children could, when the time is opportune, talk to some of the people concerned.

Follow-up
Build up a display of people who work on the street with a gallery of portraits, or a cross-section of the street with all the workers busy in the part on which they work.

Who helps whom

Age range
Seven to eleven.

Group size
Groups or class.

What you need
Paper, coloured pens or paint, scissors, adhesive, string or tape, drawing-pins.

What to do
Discuss all the people who live and work on the street. Who does what for whom? Depending on the sophistication of the children, you may want to take this to different lengths (eg residents paying rates or poll-tax to pay the wages of the council's street cleaners).

Each child then draws or paints one person, and all are mounted to form a collage. A group could paint a street background first.

Link each helper and whom they help with string and pins. Write a label explaining the nature of the help and hang this on the string.

Follow up
Keep adding people, strings and labels as new ideas come up for those who co-operate or are interdependent on the street.

Litter on the streets

Age range
Nine to eleven.

Group size
Small groups or the whole class.

What you need
Paper, pencils, clipboards.

What to do
Is the street tidy? If not, why not? Choose a stretch of street that is not very tidy, and get the class to carry out a litter survey. Allocate each group to a particular stretch (such as the space outside a house or shop).

Count up how many of each type of item is found, perhaps also showing where it was found (in one of a number of zones eg in the gutter, on the pavement, next to a building or fence etc).

It may help to draw up a tally-chart before going on the street. Discuss the likely categories first.

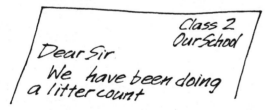

Back in class, sort out all the information. (You might use a data retrieval program with the school's microcomputer.) Where is the dirtiest place? Why? Is there any relationship between type of litter and place? Are take-away food wrappers found outside the shops concerned, or a few shops away? Why? Are bus-stops littered with used tickets?

Follow-up
What can be done about litter? The class may want to write to particular people with suggestions, such as the local council's street cleaning department, the owners of certain types of shops, or the bus company, with suggestions about raising people's consciousness about litter and perhaps providing receptacles to hold it.

Link the results to the survey of people's opinions about litter. Is there a relationship between the two?

Down the drain

Age range
Nine to eleven.

Group size
Pairs or the whole class.

What you need
A street not being used by traffic (one closed temporarily is ideal, or a cul-de-sac. The school playground will do as an alternative), spirit level, metre rule, Plasticine, paper, pencils, rulers.

What to do
Where does the rain that falls on the road go to? What would happen without the drains? Why does the water flow into them?

Look at how roads are built to have a camber and a gutter to make certain that the rain flows away. If access to a road that cars do not use is impossible, use the school playground instead.

Make a plan of the area, and measure the height on a one metre grid basis, starting at where you think is the highest point. Use the metre rule with the spirit level on top, and build up the lower end with Plasticine until the metre rule is level, with the bubble exactly in the middle. Then measure the height of the Plasticine. Remove the Plasticine, and put the other end of the metre rule on the same spot and measure on a further metre. This time, remember to add your first height of Plasticine to your second height (see Figure 1).

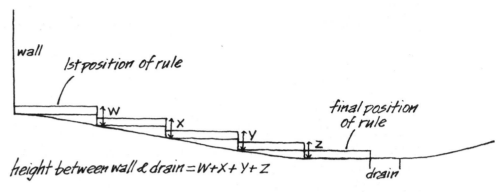

Figure 1

Eventually, you could plot quite a large area in this way, and then the whole class can combine their results in a map of the street or playground. The drains should be in the lowest points, and there should be a clear downhill run to the drains from all points. If not, puddles will form. Use the measurements to draw a side view across the road or playground. You will need to exaggerate the vertical scale at least five times.

Follow-up
It is possible, though time-consuming, to make a model of the area, using a 1 cm × 1 cm balsa strip sawn to the correct height, and stuck in a pattern on a baseboard. When firm, link each balsa pillar to its neighbours with a strip of card, and then paste down torn-up newspaper to form a surface (see Figure 2).

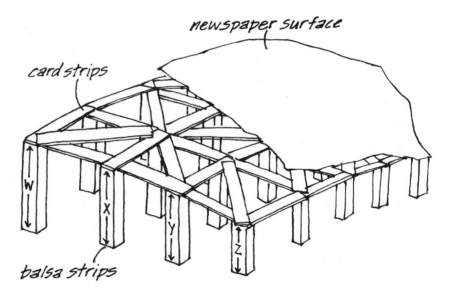

Figure 2

What do you think?

Age range
Nine to eleven.

Group size
Pairs or the whole class.

What you need
Paper, pencils, clipboard, duplicator or banda, copies of page 118.

What to do
This activity ideally follows a survey of how much litter there is on the street (see page 37). Conduct an opinion poll with members of the public to find out their attitudes to the amount of litter in the area.

You will need to discuss with the class the kinds of questions to ask first of all. It is useful to get them to realise the importance of standardised questions, and of asking questions that require the ticking of a box or entering a number, rather than writing down a comment.

Suggest that they record the sex and appropriate age of the people that they question. Point out to them that they can tell a person's sex, and make quite an accurate guess about their age, without having to ask them specific questions.

Duplicate questionnaire sheets. It is much easier to have one sheet per interview if you can afford the paper.

On the street, work in pairs. It may be interesting to record exactly where each interview takes place. For example, do people interviewed in more littered areas have more pronounced opinions?

A class of 30 can quite quickly gather 100 or more replies. Back in class, analyse the results. A microcomputer with an information retrieval (database) program would be an asset (QUEST, GRASS, DATAPROBE, KEY etc). Do women have more pronounced views than men, or older people rather than younger people? How many people want the council to provide more bins and sweepers, yet are unwilling to pay more rates or poll tax?

Follow-up
Link the results to the survey of levels of litter. Is there a relationship between the two?

Mental mapping

Age range
Five to eleven.

Group size
Individuals.

What you need
Paper, pencils, coloured pens.

What to do
Ask the children to imagine their journey to school. Can they draw a map or picture showing their route? Get them to think about the important things they go past, and to include them in their picture or plan, thinking about which side of the street they are on. Where do they turn left or right?

I turn left out of our house to Duke Street. I cross over and go down the lane at the back of the park. I go over the zebra crossing at Park Road to get to school.

Census searching

Age range
Nine to eleven.

Group size
Groups or the whole class.

What you need
Copies of the census returns for one year for a local street. 1861, 1871 or 1881 are years which usually provide good details. About six pages (150 names) will give quite enough material for a class to work on (see 'What you need' on page 27 to find out how to obtain this material).

A microcomputer with an information retrieval (database) program would be an asset (see 'What to do' on page 40 for details).

What to do
Each line of the census record gives the details for one person – where they lived, their name, age, occupation and where they were born. Records are grouped in households, so they can be used to see who used to live in each family, and in each house, over 100 years ago.

Groups of children can relate families to particular houses. Other groups can check through the records, making a tally-chart of the different occupations in the street (they may need a good dictionary for some of the descriptions), or to discover where people living on the street were born (stick self-adhesive dots on a map).

Follow-up
Get pairs of children to type the information from the census forms into a data-handling package on the microcomputer. Then the whole class can sort through the data and answer questions much more quickly and accurately.

Look at the same street ten years earlier from the previous census records, which go back to 1841, when the first census was carried out.

46	Wash Lane	1	George Wilson	Head	Mar	37		Joiner
			Eliza Do	Wife	Mar		30	Ribbon Weaver
			John E Do	Son	Unm	11		Scholar
47	do.	1	Sarah Webster	Head	W		25	Silk Winder
	do.		Emma Do	Daur	Unm		18	Cotton Weaver
			Amos Do	Son		9		Scholar
48	do.	1	Sarah Ball	Head	W		72	Midwife

A wasteland garden

Age range
Five to eleven.

Group size
Small groups.

What you need
Paper, pencils, colouring pens.

What to do
Ask the children to think about creating a small town garden for a local derelict site. Get them to think about what kind of plants and animals they want to encourage, how much it will cost to keep going, and other issues such as these.

Small groups could then draw up detailed designs.

Follow-up
Persuade the local council to look at the ideas with the children.

Shops and markets

Who shops where and when?

Age range
Five to eleven.

Group size
Pairs or small groups.

What you need
Paper, pencils, watch(es).

What to do
Find a comfortable place to overlook a small row of shops. If it can be from inside school itself, so much the better. The children keep a record of how many people enter each shop every five or ten minutes. They might make up a rota to conduct the survey over a long period.

They then graph the results and analyse them. Do all shops have a peak time for customers? Is it the same? Why are there variations?

They might ask their parents at what times they shop. They might also take their findings to the shopkeepers for their comments.

Follow-up
The survey could be extended to classify shoppers further (male or female, young or old, with or without children etc). Does this help to explain variations? Could they actually interview some of the shoppers?

A day in the life

Age range
Five to eleven.

Group size
Pairs or small groups.

What you need
Tape recorder, paper and pencils. A camera might be helpful.

What to do
Get the children to interview a series of shopkeepers about their working day. They might first discuss the kinds of day they expect the shopkeepers to have, asking questions about when they start, who cleans the shop, and other jobs which have to be done.

It is helpful if you first approach the shopkeepers, to see who is willing to be interviewed, and to find the best time to talk with them. Do try to fit in with their slack periods – it will make them much more likely to co-operate.

The children may draw up a list of questions before their interview, though it often helps not to have a specific list, but simply a number of areas to talk about – the children are then less inhibited and listen better. The questions they ask may well change as the series of interviews progresses.

Make up strip-cartoons or clock diagrams showing what happens during each hour.

Follow-up
After the children have mounted their work, invite some of the shopkeepers into school to see the results and to talk more about them.

Model shops

Age range
Five to nine.

Group size
Small groups.

What you need
Corrugated cardboard boxes, scissors, card, paper, adhesive, paint, material scraps, other junk and scrap materials.

What to do
Stick each box to form a solid cuboid, and then cut off the top and front with a pair of scissors. Get the children to decorate this as a shop front, cutting out windows and doors, adding signs etc. This should preferably be based on real observations.

Decorate the insides of each box as the inside of the corresponding shop with counters, displays, advertisements, stacks of goods, and so on, with the walls papered or painted appropriately. This too could be based on observations.

When completed, stick the insides together to form a row of shops, and the fronts of the boxes together to form a removable street-level view.

Follow-up
Older children could find out how the shops have changed from photographs and from talking to older people, and could make up a parallel model of the row of shops in the past that could be compared with the model of the present.

Origins and destinations

Age range
Nine to eleven.

Group size
Small groups or individuals.

What you need
Food labels from a variety of sources that state the country of origin, a map of the world.

What to do
Ask the children to collect foodstuff labels. In many cases, particularly of single simple products, these state the country of origin. Get children to group the products coming from particular countries. Can the children see any particular pattern? Do some groups of countries send very similar products? Are there countries which send us no foods at all?

Follow-up
Try the same process with manufactured goods. Where do these come from? Is the pattern different from foodstuffs? Why is it different?

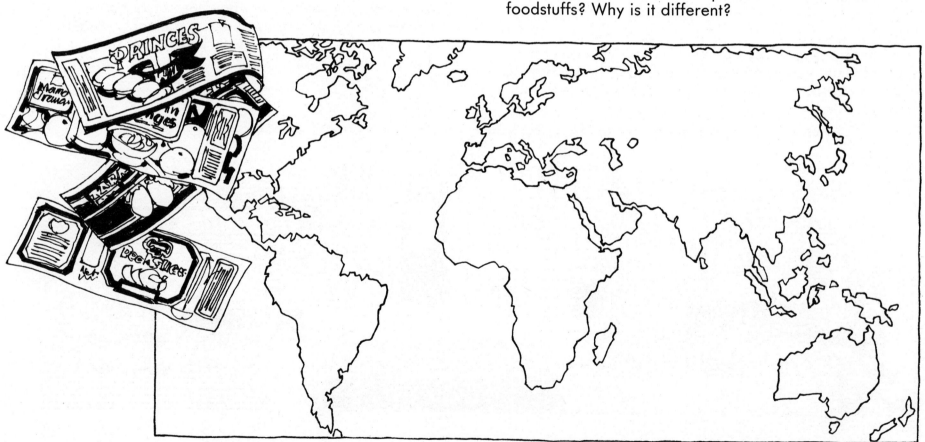

Just a spoonful of sugar

Age range
Nine to eleven.

Group size
Small groups.

What you need
Foodstuff labels, a copy of *The New E for Additives* (revised edition 1987) Maurice Hanssen (Thorsons).

What to do
Check through what is in each food. The ingredients label must list all the contents (except water) in descending order of weight. See if the children can work out the difference between a juice and a squash or a drink. What additives are used, and what do they do – preserve, add colour, or flavour?

Most additives are now listed by their E number, a Common Market scheme to classify them all.

Follow-up
Draw charts to show which foods seem to have the most additives.

Analyse the nutritional content shown on the packets of some foods. Which are the most energy-giving? Which have the lowest fat? Which are sugar-free, and how is the sweetness replaced?

Shopping zones

Age range
Nine to eleven.

Group size
Small groups.

What you need
Large scale map of the local area, tracing paper, coloured pens. A copy of the local *Yellow Pages* might also save time.

What to do
This activity works best in an area where there are several shops close to each other.

   Shops tend to be clustered together because shoppers are more likely to go to a group of shops that will between them have all that they want to buy, and perhaps also offer them some choice. On a copy of a local map, get a group to identify and colour in all the shops. How are they clustered? Where are the nearest clusters? What kind of shops are the single, isolated shops?

Follow-up
Extend this in two ways: prepare a collection of maps, showing different kinds of shops. Why are shoe shops often grouped close together? Are there particular streets that seem to have more than their share of food or clothes shops? Why do chain stores often have branches in the same small area as their rivals? (This work could be done on acetate sheets that overlap to build up a complete picture).

   Interview some shopkeepers about why their shops are where they are.

Changes

Age range
Nine to eleven.

Group size
Small groups.

What you need
Street directories (get photocopies of the relevant streets from your local library), local maps, paper and pencils.

What to do
Use the street directories to trace how a local set of shops have changed over the past years. Find the same street in each directory, and note down in columns what sort of business each shop was that year. Then look at the directory for the next year (or even five years later), and see what has happened.

Often you will find interesting changes in how things were sold. The chart below shows this:

Year	No 43	No 45
1880	Cow keeper	Milliner
1890	Cow keeper	Haberdasher
1900	Dairy	Haberdasher
1940	Dairy	Haberdasher and children's clothes
1950	Dairy	Women's and children's clothes
1960	Small grocer	Women's and children's clothes
1970	Small supermarket not in use	
1980	Large chain supermarket on both sites (and the two adjacent ones)	

Market stalls

Age range
Seven to eleven.

Group size
Small groups or the whole class.

What you need
Paper, coloured pencils, squared paper.

What to do
Visit a local street market. One of the activities could be to make a simple plan of where the different kinds of stalls are. Squared paper will help in this. You may need to discuss first the kinds of categories of stall you will use for classifying, or the children might simply list the sorts of things sold and classify back in the classroom.

Get the children to map the distribution of stalls. They will probably find very clear patterns of distribution. Why is this? Is it imposed by the market authority or for some practical reason (meat and fish stalls near running water), or do the traders choose to be like this?

Follow-up
Interview stall-holders (when trade is slackest) to find out.

Shopping in the past

Age range
Five to eleven.

Group size
Large groups or the whole class.

What you need
Any adult who can visit the class. A range of different people of a variety of ages is even better.

What to do
Find out what shops and shopping were like when this person was young. What has changed? Consider:
● types of shops,
● packaging (remember sugar in sugar-paper?),
● counters,
● tills and scales,
● shop advertising,
● shop furniture.

Follow-up
Collect photographs and books of shops in the last 100 years, and look for when and what changes have occurred.

Supermarket

Age range
Five to eleven.

Group size
Small groups.

What you need
Paper, pencil. Tape recorders and cameras would also be useful.

Follow-up
Design your own supermarkets — one to get customers to

What to do
Arrange with a local supermarket to take groups of children around the shop at a time when trade is not too busy (early afternoon might be the best time). Get the children to note where various items are stacked. They might ask the manager why these are laid out as they are.

In class discuss how the supermarket has organised things to encourage people to buy goods. Some common ploys are:

- a display of big or heavy items near the entrance (so you take a trolley rather than a basket. With a trolley, you won't notice how much you've bought);
- putting everyday things at widely dispersed parts of the shop (so to get milk, bread, vegetables and meat you will have to go past lots of shelves and displays — and be tempted);
- displays of sweets at check-out points (so children waiting with parents in the queue will ask for them).

buy a lot of goods, and the other to get customers to walk about as little as possible.

A class shop

Age range
Five to nine.

Group size
Small groups or the whole class.

What you need
A class shop, toy money, lots of things for sale.

What to do
Many classes have a play shop for imaginative play. Extend the idea and add some realistic problems for the children running the shop to solve.
- They run out of a particular line. Who do they contact to get more supplies? How much do they need? How much will it cost? What will they sell it for?
- The landlord (you) asks for the rent, the rates, the electricity payments, and so on.
- A second shop opens across the classroom — with cheaper prices!

Follow-up
The problems you are creating will make the children think about what they know about shops, though not always using adult logic. Child logic sometimes says that shops reselling goods bought from a wholesaler will make them cheaper than the buying price because they are second-hand. Don't correct them immediately: discuss shopkeeper's problems with them, or take them to talk to someone who runs a shop.

Price checker

Age range
Seven to eleven.

Group size
Small groups.

What you need
Paper, pencils, parent or other adult help.

What to do
Discuss why the same groceries cost different prices in different shops. How can they tell which shop is cheapest?

Can they devise a fair test to find out? If they are making up a basket of groceries, what will they include to be fair? Will they allow own brand goods, or insist on a well-known producer's product as the standard?

Groups can go to different shops, noting the prices and comparing the totals. Which shop is cheapest for the basket of goods?

Follow-up
Get children to examine their price lists more carefully. If they took the cheapest price of each item, how much would they save? How many shops would they have to go into? Or could they save by buying carefully at just two shops?

Repeat the exercise later in the year, and compare prices. What goods are seasonal? What non-seasonal goods have risen in price?

Ideal shops

Age range
Seven to eleven.

Group size
Small groups.

What you need
Paper, pencils, coloured pens.

What to do
What does the really perfect shop look like? Not so much outside (though they could try that too), but how would it be planned, what would it sell, what facilities would there be (for handicapped people, parents and babies etc)? When would it be open? What sort of location would be best from the consumer's point of view?

There's scope here for detailed planning and research.

ramps
toilet for the disabled
other toilets
baby changing area
créche
café
seated area
packing service

Follow-up
Work on scale designs, select furnishing styles, and build a model of the shop. Ask the public about their complaints about shops. Show the plans to a local store manager for his or her comments.

City life

Traffic census 1

Age range
Five to eleven.

Group size
Small groups.

What you need
Clipboards, squared paper.

What to do
Undertake a simple survey of different kinds of traffic, the direction in which it is going, and peak travel times.

Station a small group of children where they can see the traffic (it may be possible to do this from within the school building), and get them to compile a tally-chart of vehicles (and perhaps pedestrians as well).

They could count separately cars, buses, taxis and vans or lorries. It is probably better to choose a relatively busy street, and not to count for too long, say ten minutes. It may need more than one group, and other groups can check the traffic going in the opposite direction. Note the time carefully.

Get the children to compile bar charts. Which way is busier? Why? What vehicles are the most common? Will it be different at other times?

Follow-up
Carry the idea on to sample the traffic at one hour intervals over the school day. Does the pattern change?

What do they think might happen in the evening, at night, and at weekends?

Traffic census 2

Age range
Nine to eleven.

Group size
Small groups.

What you need
Clipboards, graph paper, coloured pens.

What to do
Extend traffic surveys to look at how traffic is organised around a set of junctions. To do this, you will need to station children to watch specific streams of traffic as they arrive at and leave various junctions. You may be able to do this with several groups of children quite close together.

You will need some way of making sure that they all monitor the traffic only between agreed times.

Analyse the data by drawing maps of traffic-flow, with the thickness of the line representing the number of vehicles (graph paper is ideal for this). Different colours can be used to show the direction traffic came from, or the map could be drawn a second time to show destinations with similar colours.

What do the maps tell the children about where traffic is flowing? How could the road junctions be replanned to allow traffic to flow more smoothly, or to interfere less with pedestrians?

Follow-up
Invite a planner from the highways division of your local authority to visit the school, who could look at the children's findings and suggestions.

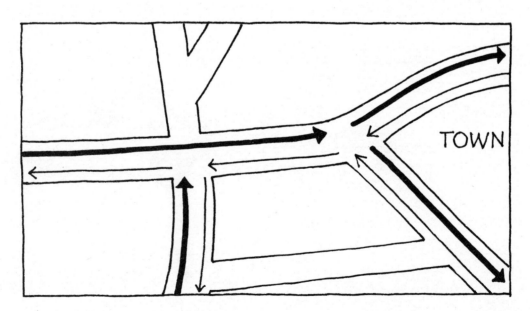

Building site

Age range
Five to eleven.

Group size
Whole class organised into groups.

What you need
A local friendly building site. Some site foremen will let children (with adequate adult supervision) on to a building site, although they will probably ask you to check with the site office first. But even from the outside of a site, you can generally see enough going on to make a visit worthwhile.

You will also need cameras, drawing paper, and tape recorders.

What to do
Building sites offer excellent examples of co-operation, interdependence, and the division of labour. Your class will be able to see specialised groups of workers who are organised in teams co-operating together.

Many sites are organised so that surveyors are still working on the final part of the buildings, while those who are laying foundations, laying bricks, plastering, decorating, and so on, are all at work on more completed parts of the site.

Look at the site. Discuss what is going on in different places, and draw and photograph different areas. See if the children can talk to workers on the site.

Follow-up
Model a building site in the classroom with modelling clay, and arrange workers in the relevant specialist groups. Get children to talk about the different skills used, and the need for teamwork and planning.

Factory

Age range
Seven to eleven.

Group size
Whole class organised into small groups.

What you need
A local factory or other workplace. Ask parents for help in finding somewhere that will let you visit.

What to do
Make a preliminary visit yourself to see what is available. Try to arrange for children to tour the prouction line, and to talk to the workers. On a first visit they will probably ask questions about the size, speed and number of operations: on a second visit they are more likely to want to talk about how the departments work together, what working life is like, and who supervises each team.

Interview a manager, an apprentice, a shop steward and a foreman.

Ask if you can collect safe scrap material from the production line. Use it for making a collage of the workplace, or for experiments on materials.

Build a model of the factory and show the line of production (this can be simplified – it does not have to be accurate).

Invite some of the workers into school to see what the class has done and to talk with them.

Archaeological dig

Age range
Seven to eleven.

Group size
Small groups.

What you need
An open space of ground that you may dig (a flower-bed of annuals is ideal after the flowering season), trowels, clipboards, small boxes etc.

What to do
Get the class to discover what happened to the flower-bed area in the past. Tell them to excavate the soil very slowly and carefully. They should mark out the area with string first, so that each find can be identified and located (position and depth), numbered, and stored (a lot of maths work is involved in this).

The first 30 cm of excavation will probably be quite jumbled because of digging for the flower-bed. Below that, there may be more of a sequence; get the children to look for layers in the wall of the excavation. They will probably find crockery fragments and general bits of rubbish. From these, try to get them to think about what must have happened, and what might have happened.

An alternative to this is for the teacher to previously bury selected items, and to choose things that might be linked together.

Follow-up
Collect together some (clean) household rubbish, and ask the children to deduce what kind of family threw this material out. Archaeologists often work on middens (rubbish tips) in this way.

Pollution tester

Age range
Five to eleven.

Group size
Whole class divided into small groups.

What you need
Various scrap material to construct testing devices.

What to do
Ask what sort of things in the area make life unpleasant. Try to get a list of pollutants, perhaps by using the senses to categorise them (noises, smells, sights).

Can the class work out ways to check how much of these there are? How bad are they? Do they vary in the immediate locality?

How do they measure noise levels? What about dirt and dust in the air? A damp white cloth in the open air, compared to a similar piece of cloth kept safely inside the classroom, may produce interesting results.

Follow-up
Plot the local levels of environmental pollution. Invite the local environmental health officer to school to discuss the children's findings with them.

Place-name search

Age range
Nine to eleven.

Group size
Small groups.

What you need
Access to copies of old maps, a local reference library.

What to do
Find out about local names – street names, pub names, local parks and open spaces.

Some of these will be based on local people and events. Others will be based on current events when the area was first being built or developed. Raglan Street, Sebastapol Terrace and Nightingale Road all refer to places or people during the Crimean War (1854–56), for example.

Use a large encyclopaedia to look up names to see if they can identify people or places, and from this identify when a place might have been named.

The local library or archive section may be able to provide more detail of local names.

Buses (times)

Age range
Seven to eleven.

Group size
Small groups.

What you need
Clipboards, watches, bus timetables, bus maps, see survey sheet on page 119.

What to do
Where do the buses that pass close to the school go? How often do they pass by? How full are they?

Get the class to organise a rota to measure how buses are used: they could look at the frequency of services (from the timetable, and measure it in real life), estimate how full passing buses are, or trace the routes and destinations of buses.

Follow-up
Conduct a survey of local people's views of the bus services. A simple questionnaire could be used at bus queues (but be prepared for interviews being cut short if the bus arrives half-way through!).

Letter-box service

Age range
Seven to eleven.

Group size
Small groups.

What you need
Clipboards, watches, a local map (large scale).

What to do
How often does the Post Office empty each local letter-box? Why do they do it at particular times? Why are letter-boxes placed where they are?

If there is a letter-box near the school, set a rota of children to monitor how many people use the box, and when. Is there a peak time? If so, is it just before the box is emptied? Is it emptied on time, early or late?

The Post Office may be interested in your findings: invite the local postmaster to school to discuss the findings. He or she will be able to tell the class about how the collections are organised.

Use a map to plot where the local letter-boxes are. Who has farthest to travel to a letter-box? Could the same number of boxes be repositioned so that the longest distance was less?

Follow-up
Try a similar survey of public telephone booths.

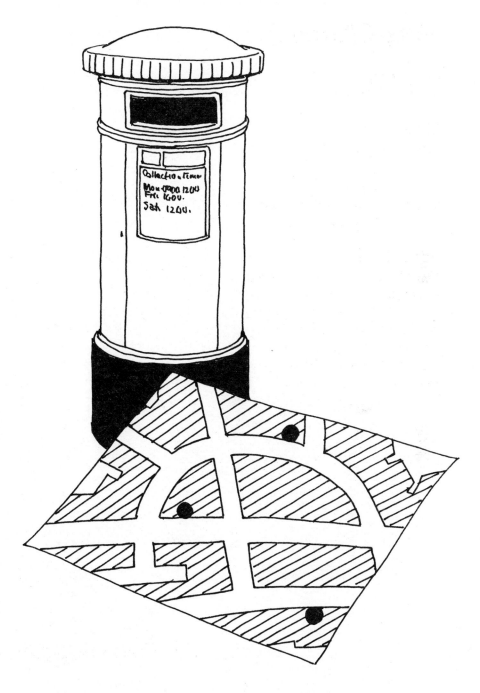

At worship

Age range
Five to eleven.

Group size
Groups or the whole class.

What you need
A local map, telephone directory.

What to do
Get the class to look at the map and find all the local places of worship. Which are churches? What denominations are they? Which are synagogues, mosques and temples?

The *Yellow Pages* may help, but not all places of worship are on the phone.

Which ones could you arrange a visit to? Most places will welcome visits from schools at times that are convenient to them. Make a visit yourself beforehand, and find out if there are any special observances that the children should respect.

Canals

Age range
Five to eleven.

Group size
Groups or the whole class.

What you need
Local map, clipboards.

What to do
Children often confuse canals and rivers: it can be worthwhile having an initial talk about the differences.

Visit a local canal, and see if children can work out how the locks operate to pass canal boats up and down. How do canals manage to have enough water to let boats pass through?

Who uses the canals today? What signs are there of how the canal was used in the past? What buildings lie alongside the canal: do they reflect its past use?

Where does the canal go? Trace its route on a map.

Railways

Age range
Seven to eleven.

Group size
Small groups or the whole class.

What you need
Clipboards, watches, copies of survey sheet on page 120.

What to do
Who uses trains from the local station? How often do trains go? Where do they go to?

Survey the local train users and ask where they are going, and note down the time. A photocopiable questionnaire can be found on page 120.

Draw a graph of when people arrive at the station, and when trains leave. How much time do people allow before their train is due to leave the station?

Draw a map to show where they go, with thicker lines to show more passengers.

Follow-up
Ask British Rail to talk with the class about their findings. How do the children think that passenger services could be improved?

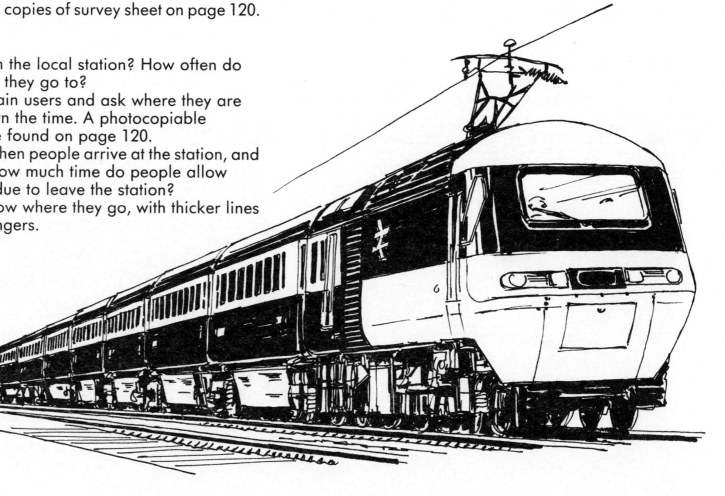

Traffic signs

Age range
Five to eleven.

Group size
Small groups or the whole class.

What you need
Paper and pencils.

What to do
Collect examples of road signs, including directional and warning signs etc.

Get the children to record what each sign looks like. Can they work out why some are circular, some rectangular, and others are triangular? Are there any other shapes?

What about the colours used on road direction signs? What is the difference between black on white, white on dark green, white on blue signs?

Follow-up
Can they design more informative road signs? Can they make signs to go around the school that will remind children not to run in the corridors?

River and sea

Floating and sinking

Age range
Five to eleven.

Group size
Whole class in small groups.

What you need
A safe river bank, sticks (some dry, some waterlogged), leaves, pebbles, other natural items.

What to do
Floating and sinking assume a new dimension in the open air. Children at the riverside will probably see a variety of items floating downstream on the water.

Encourage them to look at how some items float. Dry sticks are more buoyant than waterlogged ones; get them to look at leaves blown about on the surface by the breeze, and certain insects on the water surface. Can they classify not just what sinks and floats, but how well some things float? Can they think why there are such differences?

Only put natural items in the river for testing, unless you are certain that you can retrieve them! Look at where they float; do they seem to be caught in eddies at the side of the stream, in mid-current, or apparently against the current, if the wind is blowing upstream? Does the stream always flow in the same direction? Why? Where does it go? Where does it come from?

Follow-up
Collect some items for more detailed observation and testing in the classroom.

Try the same tests in the classroom with some seawater. Are there any differences? Why?

A seaweed weather station

Age range
Five to seven.

Group size
Class divided into small groups.

What you need
A large piece of seaweed, survey sheet on page 121.

What to do
Can you use seaweed to predict what the weather will be?

Hang up the seaweed, preferably outside in a position sheltered from the rain; otherwise inside near a window and away from a radiator. Tell the children that some people used to say that they could tell what the weather would be like by simply feeling a piece of seaweed. If it was moist and flexible, rain was due; if it was hard and dry, then the weather would be fair.

Test if this is true. How will they organise this? Remember that they will need to record their prediction, what actually happens, and whether the prediction was correct or not. This could be done with three arrows on a card, with the second and third arrow only being put in position after some time has elapsed.

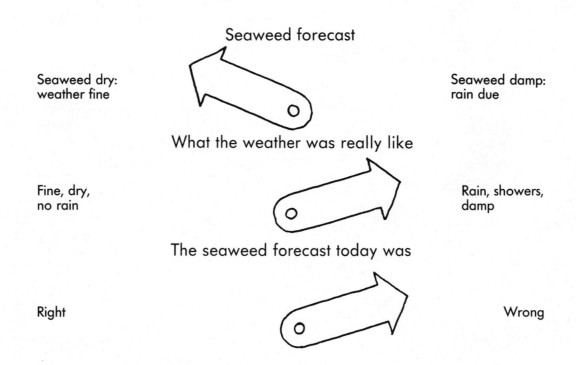

Seaweed forecast

Seaweed dry: weather fine

Seaweed damp: rain due

What the weather was really like

Fine, dry, no rain

Rain, showers, damp

The seaweed forecast today was

Right

Wrong

Filtering water

Age range
Five to seven.

Group size
Small- to medium-sized groups.

What you need
River water (preferably quite muddy), cotton wool, newspaper, some empty soft-drinks bottles (polycarbonate type).

What to do
Collect some river water and let the children look at the tiny things floating in it. There may be floating materials, mud, and small particles of sand. Can we tell what all the things are?

How is water like this made fit to drink? One of the first stages is to filter out all the larger particles.

Let the particles in the water settle during the weekend, and look for sediment. Are there layers? What seems to be in each?

Pour the water through a cotton-wool filter. Cut off the neck of a polycarbonate soft-drinks bottle to make a simple funnel. Put a wad of cotton wool in the neck, put the neck over the remainder of the bottle, and slowly pour the water through. What is different about the filtered water? Is anything caught in the cotton wool?

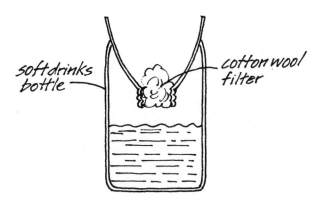

Follow-up
Try the same experiment with a filter made from blotting paper or clean newspaper. Fold a circle of paper into four, and open out one segment: drop this into the funnel. Does this filtering take as long as the cotton wool? What is collected this time?

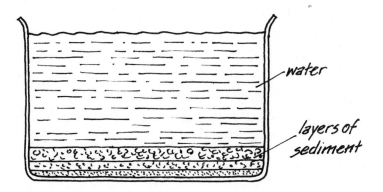

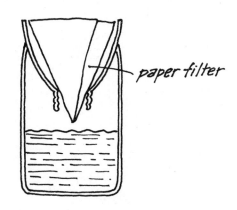

Pond dipping

Age range
Five to seven.

Group size
Small groups.

What you need
Nets (made from wire coat-hangers, garden cane, the feet of pairs of tights, plastic jars), white enamel trays.

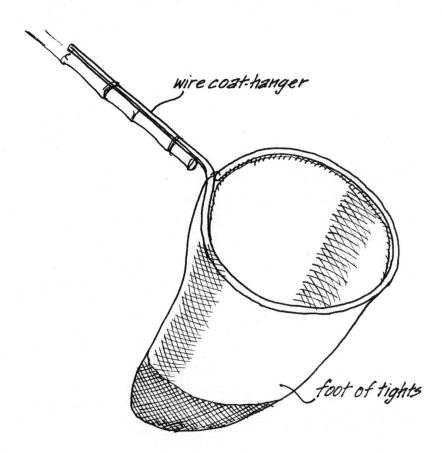

wire coat-hanger

foot of tights

What to do
Shop-bought nets are usually too coarse to catch anything but small fish. Finer nets can easily be made from the feet of old tights, supported by a wire loop made from a coat-hanger.

Put some water in the enamel tray. Scoop in the pond or river for anything that looks interesting, and empty the contents into the tray. Because it is white, it is easier to see what has been found, and the water supports the animals and plants so that they can be seen properly.

What do the children find? Can they classify things into animals and plants? Sort each type of animal into different jars.

Before leaving the pond or river area, carefully empty the jars and trays back into the pond. Explain why it is important not to remove living things — plants or animals — from ponds and rivers.

Follow-up
Draw what has been found.

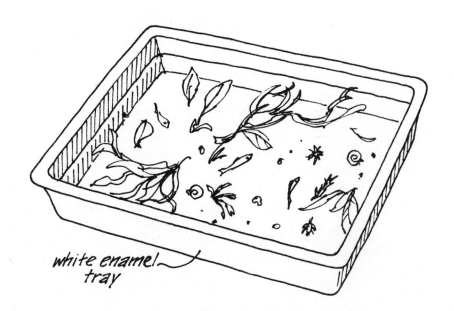

white enamel tray

Skimming

Age range
Seven to nine.

Group size
Individuals or small groups.

What you need
A clear stretch of river or an empty beach; lots of flattish stones.

What to do
How can the children make the stones bounce on the water? Show them how to skim the stones, making them spin horizontally on the surface of the water as they are thrown. Some of the children will soon be doing this better than you!

   How many bounces can they get from one stone? How heavy a stone can they skim? Does the weight make a difference?

Follow-up
Try other variations to test what makes skimming possible. Does it help if you are lower down to the water surface, or higher up? What happens if the stone is spun around a different axis or if the stone is more spherical?

River currents

Age range
Seven to nine.

Group size
Small groups.

What you need
Paper, pencils, small twigs.

What to do
Get the children to look at how a stream flows. Where does it go faster? Where does the water seem to go in currents?

Get them to check where the water flows by dropping in small twigs and seeing where they float. As the currents move about in the river, so the twigs will be carried about.

Get the children to draw (or draw for them) a plan of part of the stream. By dropping twigs in different parts of the river (say one midstream, one to the left bank, and one to the right), they can follow where the water current in that part of the stream goes, and plot this on their map.

Can they detect a pattern in the different currents? Can currents cross over?

Follow-up
If the stream is small, they may be able to look at the different depths of water, and relate this to the strengths of current.

By releasing several twigs together in different currents, they can compare the times of each one.

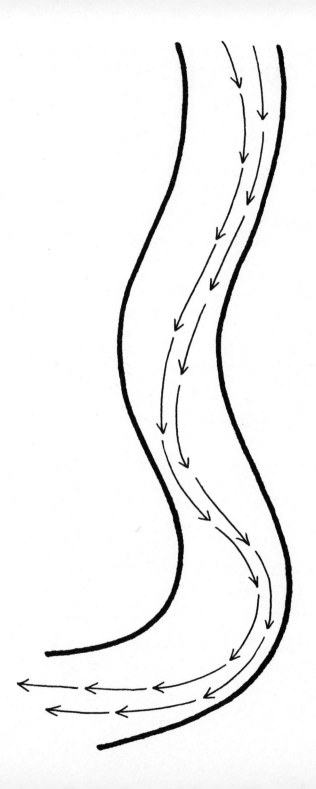

People using the river

Age range
Seven to nine.

Group size
Small groups or the whole class.

What you need
A river bank, and time to walk along it.

What to do
Walk along a river bank, taking particular note of who is using the river. Children could look for people they can see doing something – fishing, river police, conservation work.

They may be able to talk with some of the people that they meet (though not all anglers would welcome this).

An important aspect of river use today is for leisure. Are there examples of this use in your survey?

Follow-up
Look at the changing patterns of use of the river. Who used it, and for what? Signs that people have used or are using the river include footpaths, and disused water-wheels.

When the boat comes in

Age range
Five to eleven.

Group size
Small- to medium-sized groups.

What you need
Plenty of time at a coastal location, a pair of binoculars.

What to do
Survey the boat and ship traffic in a port, estuary, or from the beach.

What kinds of ship are passing? Can you tell what they are carrying, or do they have some other purpose, such as fishing, or part of a navy? Can you tell the routes that they have followed by buoys in the water?

Follow-up
Try to visit a dock to see goods being loaded and unloaded.

Beach scavenging

Age range
Seven to nine.

Group size
Small groups or individuals.

What you need
A fairly clear beach, just after high tide.

What to do
First check that the beach is pollution-free.

Explain that they are going to try to find out about how the seas in the local area are used by looking for signs of human activity that have been washed up on the shore.

Working in pairs or individually, they must look along the high-water mark for items of interest, each having a particular stretch to search. You might discuss why the high-water mark is significant.

Can they tell what has been happening on the beach and off-shore from what they find? Fragments of fishing net, old cans, empty containers, rubbish from ships, rope, and wood all help piece together ideas.

Follow-up
Can they classify things from ships into flotsam and jetsam? Flotsam is wreckage from a ship (so things like old fishing floats and nets would count), while jetsam is thrown overboard (old containers, for example).

River patterns

Age range
Nine to eleven.

Group size
Small groups.

What you need
Either a beach with a small clean streamlet flowing down it, or a long sand tray along which you can let water flow (see Figure 1).

What to do
Rivers form their shapes by eroding their banks in some places, and depositing silt in others. It is quite easy for children to model this happening. Letting a stream of water flow across a sloping sand surface will cut a river bed as it flows along.

By making a twisting path for the river, children can observe the erosion that takes place on the outer part of bends, and the deposition on the inner parts. Adding sand of a slightly different colour to the stream will make this even more obvious. They will see the sand build up in the shallows, and be cut away from where the deeper and stronger currents flow. The bends will gradually become more and more pronounced: eventually, the bends may link up and sections of the original river bed will be bypassed.

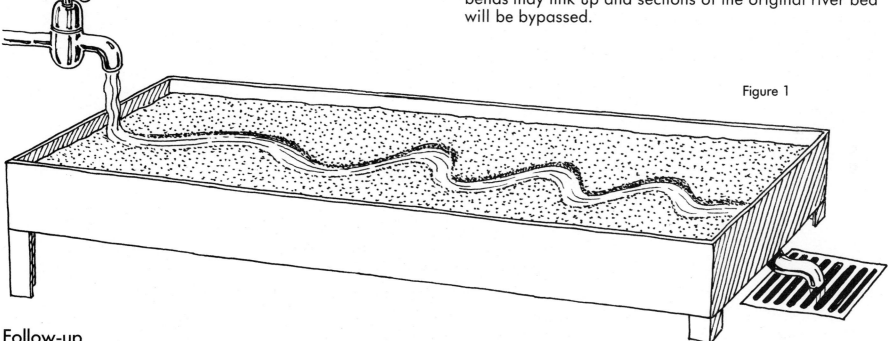

Figure 1

Follow-up
Look at a real river for signs of erosion and deposition. Photographs of large rivers will also be helpful.

Seasonal change

Age range
Nine to eleven.

Group size
Whole class.

What you need
Access to either a river or a beach at a number of times over the year.

What to do
Most children only know the seaside in summer, and probably see less of rivers in the winter months. Try making regular visits to the same river or beach over the whole year.

There will be changes to look for in:
- how humans use the area, such as seasonal leisure activities and seasonal work;
- plant life changes;
- changing animals, with migratory birds in particular; but also important changes in insect life.

Follow-up
Chart the changes in the classroom. Mount a display of photographs and samples, perhaps in some circular form, or right around the room, to show the cyclical nature of these changes.

Pollution

Age range
Nine to eleven.

Group size
Small groups or the whole class.

What you need
Paper, pencils, clipboards, sample tubes.

What to do
Survey all the rubbish and litter along the banks of the river. Children should be asked not to touch anything, merely to observe and note.

One group should look for solid rubbish, noting what they find and where it is situated. A second group should look at the condition of the water. They could look for signs of petrol or oil on the surface, and for detergent foam, and take samples of the water to see how clear it is (make sure that this group is *closely* supervised). A third group could look for signs of animal and plant life, or the lack of it.

In class, the various groups can try to correlate their different findings.

Follow-up
The same approach could be used along a stretch of beach.

Food chains

Age range
Nine to eleven.

Group size
Small groups or whole class.

What you need
Nets (made from the feet of tights, coat-hangers and garden cane, see page 76), plastic jars.

What to do
Older junior children can take pond-dipping to greater lengths than younger children.

Collect as many different forms of plant and animal life as possible from the pond. Put each in separate jars.

Back in class, draw and, if possible, identify each plant and animal. Label each jar, then find out what each animal eats. This will allow the children to build up for themselves a food chain, from plants to the largest predator. There may be more than one chain, and each may branch, one animal having a diet of several species in the layer below. However, not all of these may be apparent.

Remember to firstly take enough pond water to keep the plants and animals alive during the period of the experiment, and, secondly, to return all water and surviving plants and animals to the pond afterwards.

Follow-up
Make a mobile of animal and plant shapes that demonstrates the food chain.

Tides

Age range
Seven to eleven.

Group size
Any size.

What you need
A watch, a beach.

What to do
This activity is suitable for a school trip to the seaside. Simply get the children to note down when the tide is fully in and fully out. This may call for some investigation on the beach to try and work out how to tell high-tide and low-tide – it isn't easy, and some estimation may be needed.

If there are suitable rocky landmarks, they could also find out how far out the tide goes: it's easier to tell how high it comes from the tide mark.

Do this over a few days. Many children from inland are surprised that high tide isn't at the same time each day, and that the high-water mark seems to be getting regularly higher or lower, as the spring and neap tides alternate over a four-week cycle.

Follow-up
Once they have established that tides seem to be getting an hour or so earlier each day, see if they can predict the times of high-tides.

Discuss why tides occur (the gravitational pull of the moon from 250,000 miles away) and the enormous power that is there every day. Back in school, how might this power be harnessed?

Village and country

Hedgerows

Age range
Seven to nine.

Group size
Groups or the whole class.

What you need
An identification key for plants.

What to do
Hedgerows are a disappearing part of our countryside, and some of them are surprisingly old, dating back before the Norman Conquest.

A way of estimating the age of a hedge is to count the different species of plant that make it up. For every species beyond the first, the hedge is approximately 100 years old, so a seven-species hedge probably dates from around 1400.

Get groups to try to identify how many species there are in some hedges. Ask them to avoid cutting the hedge to remove samples, or damaging it in any other way.

Follow-up
A really ambitious class project would be to map the hedges with different colours showing different ages.

How would this compare to large scale historical maps of the area?

Village changes

Age range
Seven to eleven.

Group size
Small groups or the whole class.

What you need
Cameras, tape recorders, clipboards, pencils.

What to do
Village life is changing rapidly. Get the class to jot down what they expect to find in a country village before they go. You will probably get a rather idyllic picture of rural England. Then visit the village to look at what it is really like. You might get the children to think of questions that they could ask local people about village life.

Look at how the houses have changed by the addition of telephone wires, electricity mains, and slate roofing. Ask about services — many town children will not realise that rural areas do not always have mains gas, or even mains sewage. What range of shops is there? What is the local transport like?

Follow-up
For more ideas on village shops and transport, see pages 98 to 99.

Domesday survey

Age range
Seven to eleven.

Group size
Any size.

What you need
A large scale local map (1:10,000), clipboards and pencils. Access to either the BBC Domesday Project data on your area (on the Interactive video disc system: your LEA will be able to advise you on where the nearest set of equipment can be found); or a copy of the original 1086 version (your nearest large library should have a copy of the translation for your county, published by Phillimore).

What to do
Get the children to find out what your area looked like, either in 1086 or 1986. Remember that the 1086 Domesday survey was essentially a survey of taxable wealth made for the colonial state, while most of the local data in the 1986 survey is an impressionistic account of the area.

What can be found that is the same or is different? You may want to make a detailed comparison of land-use in the area (most of which will not have changed since 1986), or changes in some of the amenities.

Could the class construct their own follow-up survey, using either 1086 or 1986 as a model?

Follow-up
Date and keep any data the children collect in school. It could be very useful to a teacher in a few years' time, who will then have yet another survey to use for comparison!

On the farm

Age range
Five to eleven.

Group size
Groups or the whole class.

What you need
Cameras, tape recorders, clipboards etc.

What to do
What happens on a farm? Who works there?

These two seemingly straightforward questions will prompt a bizarre and often incorrect collection of information from most town-dwelling children. The idea of a farm being a work place, run to produce livestock or crops (sometimes both), seems not to have occurred to many of them. So when you get them down on the farm, try getting the children to ask people what jobs they do (when they start in the morning; if it is the same throughout the year; what machinery they use). Find out how farmers decide what animals to keep, and what crops to grow.

Follow-up
How many people worked on the same farm in the past: how do they do the same or more work now with much fewer people?

90

Plant survey

Age range
Nine to eleven.

Group size
Pairs.

What you need
Metre rules, skewers or pegs, string, clipboards, throwing frames. (A throwing frame is a hollow square, usually 30 cm square*, used to toss on the ground to select an area for a survey. They are usually made of stiff wire or hardboard.)

What to do
Select a small area to survey. It is a good idea to find an area with some variation in it – perhaps from under the trees to a more open space, or the banks of a stream. The object is to get the class to accurately plot how plants are distributed.

Get the children to mark out an area, perhaps 3 metres by 15 metres, using the string and pegs. Use a combination

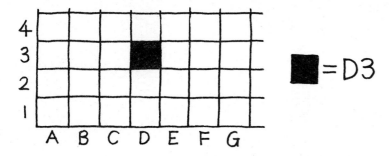

*If you make the square with 31.6 cm sides, then each sample frame gives you exactly one-tenth of a square metre. This makes calculations considerably easier.

of letters and numbers to identify each square.

Each pair of children is allocated a square, throws the frame on it, and then counts up the number of a particular plant within the frame. You will need to select which plants to look for beforehand, and make sure all the children can recognise them. They then record the number of plants in their square, and then sample a second area. When all the squares are surveyed, the class can look for patterns, and suggest reasons. They could then survey a second or third plant type, and see if all plants show the same distribution.

Follow-up
This will also work with minibeasts. The information could be used in a database program with a microcomputer (details on page 40).

Fossil dig

Age range
Nine to eleven.

Group size
Small groups or the whole class.

What you need
Each child will need a hammer (you will need as many adults as possible for a trip of this nature), clipboards and pencils.

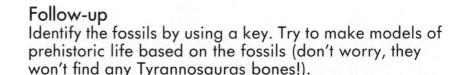

What to do
Make a preliminary survey to find a suitable outcrop of rock, or a disused quarry (chalk or soft limestone are good for young children). Geography teachers in a local secondary school may be able to help.

The children will need to be shown safe ways of using their hammers to crack rocks, and be given careful safety rules concerning disused quarries.

Get the class to record where they make their finds. This information could be plotted to show likely areas in which to find more fossils, and also to look at the distribution of the different kinds of fossils.

Follow-up
Identify the fossils by using a key. Try to make models of prehistoric life based on the fossils (don't worry, they won't find any Tyrannosauras bones!).

Orienteering

Age range
Nine to eleven.

Group size
Pairs.

What you need
Compasses (for direction).

What to do
Plot a simple, short route over an area of heath or commonland, perhaps 300–400 metres for a first attempt. Describe the route to the children using distances and compass directions (30 paces north, 50 paces north-east, etc). Can they finish at the end-point you chose?

Follow-up
Use LOGO on the microcomputer for the same purpose. Can they plot a route on screen? This creates particular problems because the LOGO turtle has its direction fixed on a relative basis, but it is a problem that children are likely to be able to solve.

Soils

Age range
Seven to eleven.

Group size
Twos and threes.

What you need
Soil testing kits (from gardening shops), trowels, containers, accurate scales (preferably to at least the nearest half-gram), clipboards, pencils.

What to do
Soils differ from each other. Get the class to collect samples from different places, and put them in plastic containers or bags. They can then test different samples for acidity (using the soil testing kit). Are the plants from the area with acid soil different from those with alkali soil?

Try weighing out a sample of soil, and then letting it dry completely. Reweigh it to find the water content. Do some soils retain more water than others?

Put a sample of each soil in a jam jar, add water and shake, and then leave it for some hours to settle. Which soils have more small stones or sand? Which have more fine silt or clay or floating humus?

Directions (natural compasses)

Age range
Seven to eleven.

Group size
Any size.

What you need
An analogue watch (ie not digital), a magnetic compass (to check).

What to do
There are many ways to tell directions without using the conventional magnetic compass. Moss usually grows on the bark of trees on the shaded, north side. The grass is often greener and lusher on the north slope of a hill, where water has evaporated less.

Can the class use signs like this to tell direction? What other signs can they find?

You can also use a watch to tell direction. Point the hour hand in the direction of the sun. The direction south lies on the line between the hour hand and the 12 o'clock line. This works correctly for GMT: use the 1 o'clock line during summertime.

Follow-up
What rules will apply in the southern hemisphere?

River profile

Age range
Nine to eleven.

Group size
Small groups or whole class.

What you need
A simple flora chart to identify common plants identification charts for insects, measuring tape, clipboards.

What to do
Get the children to record accurately how the plant and animal life change near a river or stream. A cross-section of the river will require the children to carefully plot where different kinds of plants are to be found. It may help to peg out string to the bank of the stream so that distances can be measured. Throwing frames (page 91) could be used.

The other kind of river profile is a section drawn down the length of the stream. This involves noting how the slope of the river bed changes. Generally rivers slope more (and run faster) nearer their source, and slope less and flow more slowly nearer the sea. But this isn't always the case. Children could plot this for a short stream.

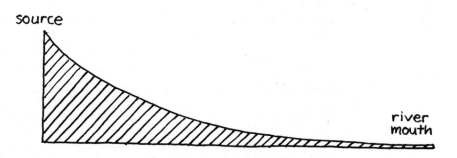

source

river mouth

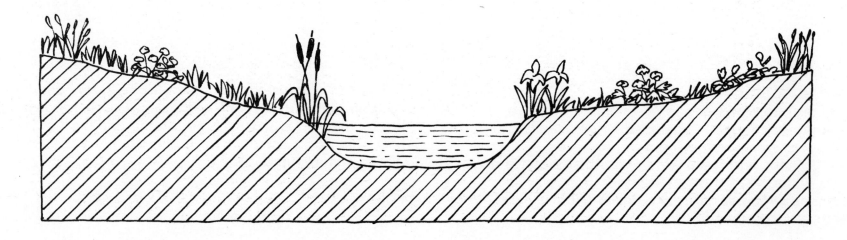

How high is the tree?

Age range
Nine to eleven.

Group size
Small group.

What you need
Tape measure, string, card, paper-fasteners, weight eg cotton reel, copies of template on page 122 and 123.

What to do
Get the children to estimate the height of various trees. Then ask them to calculate the heights, to see how accurate they are.

A simple method is to measure the length of shadow of a known height (a child or a teacher, for example) and then compare this to the tree's shadow.

A clinometer can be made from card and string, as well as being bought from mathematical suppliers. By standing at a fixed distance from a tree trunk, and pointing the pointer at the tree top, the weighted string can be used as a marker to indicate the height of the tree.

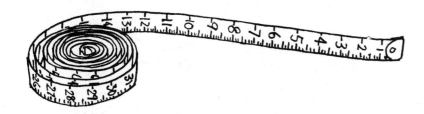

Follow-up
Do the children think their skill of estimating improves as they measure heights? How could they find out?

The back of beyond

Age range
Nine to eleven.

Group size
Class discussion, small groups for work.

What you need
Photocopied pages of a high-scale map*, coloured pencils, ruler.

What to do
Make copies of a large scale map of a countryside area, preferably one that the children already know or will be visiting. Discuss what makes an area really cut off. Is it distance from roads, or from shops, or a bus route? There are lots of areas for discussion about how places can be isolated from the outside world.

Get the children to use the maps to find out where is the most remote area. They could, for example, shade in all the area within a mile of a bus route, or within the distance of a bus stop.

What about roads, phone boxes, post offices and railways? For each of these, decide how important they are for keeping in touch with a locality. There may be some difficult decisions to make; motorways, for example, can often cut off rural areas more than they improve access.

The children's maps will eventually show all the isolated areas unshaded. Which is the largest? Is it possible to visit it?

*Check that your LEA or school has copyright permission to make photocopies of published maps.

Follow-up
Try the same activity in an urban area: you will need to use different criteria, of course, but can still find out which parts of a city are most cut off from the centre.

The village shop

Age range
Five to eleven.

Group size
Small groups.

What you need
Clipboard and pencils.

What to do
Study how a small village shop differs from shops in town. What sorts of things does it stock? Why does it have some ranges that are not found in other places? Does it have a wide variety? What sort of prices does it charge? Why are prices different from town shops? Is it combined with a post office?

Interview the shopkeeper. What can she or he tell you about the shop? How long has it been there? Who uses it? When is it open? What has changed in the past five, ten, or 20 years?

Conduct a survey of shop use. How many people come to it? When? How do they travel? Do they buy many items, or just a few?

Public transport

Age range
Seven to eleven.

Group size
Small group.

What you need
Local maps.

What to do
How do people travel around country areas?

Get the class to look at local bus patterns. They may be surprised at how infrequently buses visit the villages — sometimes there are only buses once or twice a week in rural areas. Where do the buses go? How long can people have in the town shops before they have to get the bus back?

Ask local people about how things have changed. Why are there fewer buses? What alternate methods do people use nowadays?

Around the year

How much snow?

Age range
Nine to eleven.

Group size
Groups.

What you need
Rectangular plastic trays, buckets, measuring jugs, balance and weights, metre rules, a calculator.

What to do
What is the volume of snow that has fallen in the playground? How much water does this represent? How heavy would this be?

Leave a plastic tray in the playground overnight to collect the snow. Alternatively, lightly scoop the snow into the tray, trying not to compress it. Many schools have work trays for children; these are ideal for catching snow, and their dimensions are often 33 cm – 25 cm – 10 cm, which makes calculations very easy, as 12 together make a square metre.

Bring the snow into the class to melt. What is the volume now? Measure and weigh it.

Measure the depth of snow in the playground at several points: work out an average depth. Measure the area of the playground, and then calculate the volume of snow. What size snowman would this make? How heavy would all that snow be?

Follow-up
The results can be surprising. Go on to calculate the strain put on roofs etc.

Snowflakes

Age range
Seven to eleven.

Group size
Individuals.

What you need
Hand lenses, small sheets of glass or perspex, black paper.

What to do
Catch and look at snowflakes.

Leave the glass or perspex out in the cold for half an hour first – the colder it is, the less likely the snowflakes will melt. Tape the black paper on to the underside of the glass, to give a strong contrasting background.

Each snowflake is always based on a hexagonal pattern, and all six axes are symmetrical. There are so many variations possible that no two snowflakes are identical.

Measuring the rainfall

Age range
Seven to eleven.

Group size
Rota of pairs or small groups.

What you need
Measuring cylinder, funnel, empty polycarbonate drinks bottle, copies of page 124.

What to do
It always surprises children to know how small an amount of rain actually falls. If you ask them to estimate how much has fallen after a heavy rainstorm, you will rarely get estimates of less than a centimetre, which is the most it usually is. The depth of puddles is probably a confusing factor.

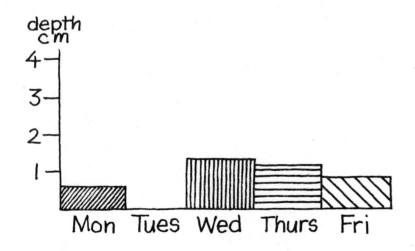

A rain gauge can be simply constructed from an empty plastic (polycarbonate) drinks bottle – the wider the diameter the better. Cut off the top and invert it to make a funnel (this helps minimise evaporation).

A measuring cylinder can be made from a straight-sided receptacle (the narrower the better). The simplest way to develop a scale is to pour 2 cm of water into your collecting cylinder, and then tip this into your measuring cylinder. Mark the height the water reaches, and then calculate the intermediary positions.

Leave the collecting cylinder out in the same position for 24 hours. (Children could experiment with more than one cylinder in a variety of positions to see why this is important.) Measure the rain level each day at the same time. Weekends will be a problem.

Follow-up
Keep a histogram chart of the results.

Keep a note of rainfall figures in a daily newspaper, and/or compare the local Met Office rain record with your own. How much do they differ?

Sun and cloud

Age range
Nine to eleven.

Group size
Pairs in rota.

What you need
Light-sensitive ozalid paper, a stout cardboard box, black paper, adhesive.

What to do
Younger children can keep a rough visual record of how sunny it is, and this can be quite a useful introduction to the following process for older children.

Recording how much actual sunshine there is can be more difficult. A rota of children could simply monitor the sky with a watch, timing the gaps between clouds. A less boring and more sophisticated method is by using a crude pin-hole camera.

A simple cardboard box, preferably of two interlocking halves, is lined with black paper. A pin-hole (actually a hole about 3 mm in diameter) is made in the middle of the end of the large box.

In the dark (or at least subdued light), load light-sensitive paper into the bottom of the smaller box, and assemble both boxes. Place the camera in the open, away from shadow or trees, with the pin-hole uppermost.

At the end of the day, the sun (when it is out) will have traced an exposure over the light-sensitive paper. Clouds will have prevented sufficient light from making a mark. It is possible to measure how much sun there was, although the scale is not straightforward, and may need some form of experimentation to get a reasonably accurate record.

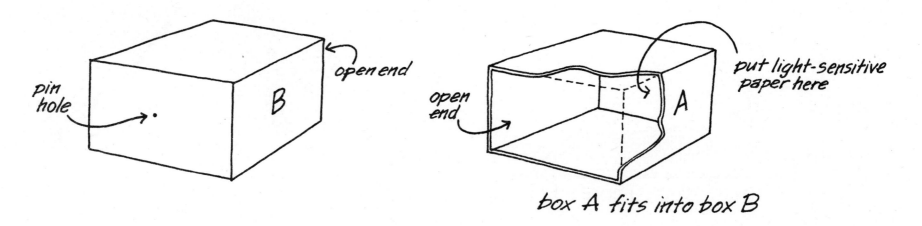

pin hole

open end

B

open end

put light-sensitive paper here

A

box A fits into box B

Wind direction

Age range
Seven to eleven.

Group size
Pairs in rota or the whole class.

What you need
Weather-vane (made from plywood, with a needle or a round nail in a cork as an axis), a compass, copies of page 125.

What to do
Construct the weather-vane and place it well off the ground, in a place that can be seen from the classroom window.

How often and when should observations be made? This will be an interesting class discussion. You might initially have a series of observations every five minutes, and from this help build up the idea of a prevailing wind. Are there particular times of the day when it is better to read the wind direction?

Results are traditionally recorded on a wind rose (see page 125): use a fresh rose each month, and either shade in or write the date in boxes radiating from the centre. Different months can then be compared.

wind rose

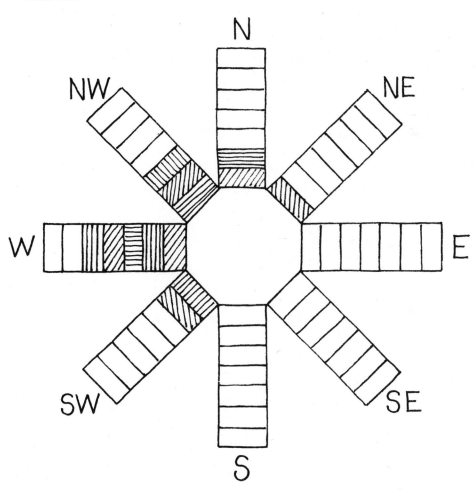

Weather lore

Age range
Five to eleven.

Group size
Individual to whole class.

What you need
Pencils and paper.

What to do
There is an enormous range of folk sayings about the British weather. The following list contains some of the best known ones:

- Red sky at night, shepherd's delight;
  Red sky in the morning, shepherd's warning.
- If it rains on St Swithin's Day (15th July), it will rain for the next 40 days.
- Rain before seven, fine by eleven.
- Too cold to snow.
- Full moon, frost soon.
- Clear sky, frost nigh.
- The north wind doth blow,
  And we shall have snow.

Get the children to:

- collect as many sayings as possible;
- try to find ways of testing them to see if they work or not;
- try to work out if there is any reason why the sayings should be true.

Follow-up
Do other countries have similar collections of weather lore? (They may not – one reason why the British Isles are so rich in sayings is because our weather is so variable.) Children can collect sayings from other countries (particularly children from non-English backgrounds) by asking parents and relatives.

Wet play

Age range
Seven to eleven.

Group size
Pairs or small groups.

What you need
Nothing specific.

What to do
Two questions, the answers to which might at least prove interesting in the staff room!

● How many 'wet plays' are there, and when do they occur?
● What do children like to do during 'wet play'?

Pairs of children could then survey the other classes. Make sure that they discuss how to get a balanced sample by covering all the ages and both sexes.

Follow-up
Ask the class to draw up plans for activities for wet playtimes for each class, bearing in mind how often they may happen.

Measuring the temperature

Age range
Seven to eleven.

Group size
Rota of pairs.

What you need
Thermometer, paper for recording, copies of page 126.

What to do
A rota of children collect maximum and minimum temperatures each day. It is best to let the same pair work together for a whole week, as they will probably need time to get used to the scale, and the way of reading the thermometer.

Discuss the variation in temperature over the day. You could get children to record the temperature at shorter intervals — say every half-hour — for a day or so.

The thermometer's position is important. Conventionally, it should be stationed about one metre off the ground in a shaded spot. Can the class work out why? If this does give regular readings, perhaps a child could take the thermometer home at weekends so that more continuous records can be maintained.

Follow-up
Use the temperature records collected alongside other weather data: are there patterns linking rain, cloud, and temperature? There is always lots of interesting maths to be done with records like this: for example, the children could try to find the biggest gap between maximum and minimum readings, average temperatures, and so on.

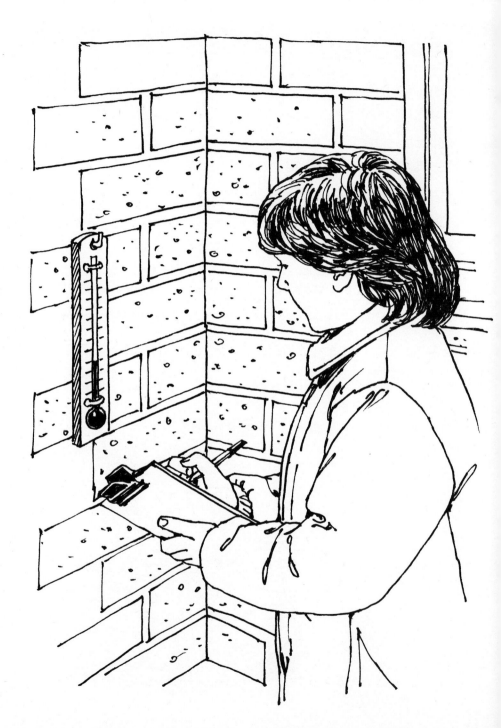

Conkers

Age range
Seven to eleven.

Group size
Small groups to whole class.

What you need
Conkers, one gram weights, scales, measuring cylinders to measure cubic centimetres (cc), and perhaps varnish, vinegar etc.

What to do
As the conker season begins, ask the children what sort of conker is the strongest. You will get replies that include natural characteristics (heavy, large, old etc.) and those that involve special treatments or recipes (baking slowly in an oven, a week's immersion in vinegar, layers of varnish).

Get the children to collect conkers and test out the different claims to strength. How will they measure strength? They might drop the conkers, drop weights on them, or perhaps measure how many conkers can be squeezed in a woodworking vice before they crack.

Follow-up
Use an information handling program on the school's microcomputer to help analyse and process the children's results (see page 40 for details).

Leaf-fall

Age range
Seven to eleven.

Group size
Small groups or the whole class.

What you need
Fairly regular access to a collection of different types of trees.

What to do
In September, get the children to identify the different varieties of trees, then encourage them to carefully and regularly note the changes in the leaves of each variety over the early autumn. Which varieties of tree change colour first? Which fall first? How long does it take for all the leaves to fall? Do all trees of the same family behave in the same way?

What do the children think causes the leaves to fall?

Follow-up
There is also a wealth of creative work, such as painting, collage, patterns, and colour mixing, that can spring from the colours and patterns of leaves in autumn.

Seeds

Age range
Five to eleven.

Group size
Any size.

What you need
Access to a variety of plants.

What to do
Collect a range of different seeds. Get the children to examine each and decide how they think they are scattered. Discuss why seeds need to be scattered in the first place.

Can the class form different categories for dispersal methods? Which are the best shapes for air-borne seeds? Which seeds depend on animals? Do they rely on specific types of animal?

Which seed dispersal systems are most effective? How can this be tested?

Beanstalk

Age range
Seven to eleven.

Group size
Rota of children over two or three weeks.

What you need
Beans, plastic bottles (with top cut off), stones, blotting paper, ruler(s).

What to do
Grows beans or peas in a jar with blotting paper. Get the children to measure, as accurately as possible, the length of the main root and the main shoot each day. Use a tall plastic bottle, well weighted with stones, and fix a metre rule, marked in millimetres, next to the bean before you start.

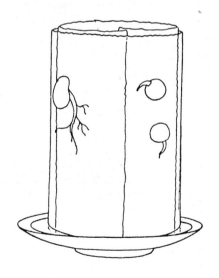

Get the children to draw a block graph of the growth. Which is greatest? When? Why? Do plants growing in soil display the same pattern?

Follow-up
How do plants grow – steadily, or in bursts? How fast do they grow? Does anything make them grow faster or slower?

Holidays

Age range
Five to nine.

Group size
Whole class.

What you need
Some artefacts from your own holiday, such as a postcard, a pebble, a shell, a ticket.

What to do
Start a class collection of things brought back from holiday. This can be deliberately keyed to include all those who did not 'go away' on holiday.

Get children to mark their holidays on a suitable scale map. Who travelled most? Who travelled least?

Seasonal work

Age range
Seven to eleven.

Group size
Any size.

What you need
No special requirements.

What to do
Over the year, get the children to look out for and collect information about people who do particular jobs in different seasons. This may be seasonal work (eg footballers, a store's Santa), or people whose work varies with the seasons (a park gardener).

Create a frieze of the months of the year and get individual children to draw and paint all the different kinds of work appropriate to each season.

Discuss why the work varies. Is there any particular season that seems busier than another? Who is busy when someone else is slack?

Follow-up
Get children to ask parents and relatives about seasonal variations in their work. What problems and advantages does this bring?

Hot air balloons

Age range
Nine to eleven.

Group size
Whole class (small groups to start).

What you need
Good quality tissue-paper (at least eight large sheets), diluted PVA adhesive, thin wire, pliers, a cannister gas stove or a blowtorch, fine string, empty tin cans.

What to do
Get the class to construct a large hot air balloon. Cut out eight to twelve panels from the sheets of tissue-paper. The shape in the diagram (Figure 1) should be used, but the angle at the top will depend on the number of sheets used. The objective is to get a flattish top, so eight sheets will need an angle of 45°, ten an angle of 36°, and twelve of 30°.

Figure 1

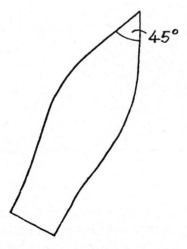

The sheets should be stuck together with dilute PVA adhesive, using as little as possible, but leaving no holes, and with very little overlap. The bottom should be left free, and a thin wire circle, about 30 cm in diameter, glued in place (Figure 2).

Figure 2

On a fairly windless cold day, carefully inflate the balloon. Use a chimney of tin cans (tops and bottoms removed) to funnel hot air from the stove to the neck of the balloon (Figure 3). Have the balloon tethered by thin string.

As the balloon fills, it will slowly rise against the tether. When it is fully inflated, allow the stove to heat the air for a few minutes further before letting the balloon rise.

Figure 3

Why is this a seasonal activity? In summer, the difference in temperature inside and outside the balloon will be less, and the buoyancy may not even be enough to achieve take-off.

Wind strength

Age range
Seven to eleven.

Group size
Pairs or small groups.

What you need
Cardboard boxes (eg soap powder), scissors, string or tape.

What to do
The speed of the wind can be measured using, at one extreme an anemometer (a fairly expensive device of spinning half-cups linked to a measuring device), and at the other, simple observations linked to the locality. The Beaufort scale, for example, provides a link between what is happening in the environment and the speed of the wind. See page 127 for the whole scale.

Between these extremes, this simple device can be made and calibrated using the Beaufort scale. The hinged flap is either suspended by a string tied between the two sides of the box, or taped to the top: either way, it should be free enough to swing in the wind. The flap should be cut so that the side will show on the scale.

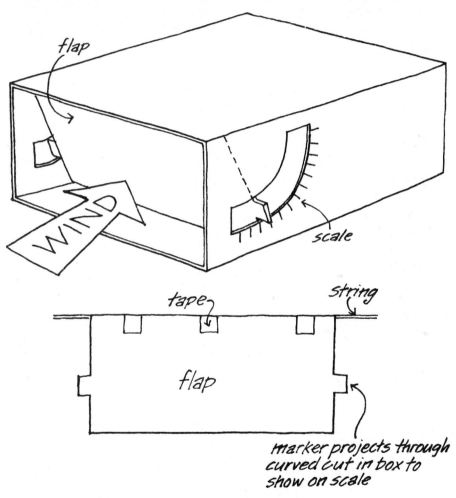

marker projects through curved cut in box to show on scale

To use this, simply point the box into the wind and note the degree to which the flap is lifted by it.

Reproducible material

Litter survey

	Yes	No
1 Is litter a problem at school?	☐	☐
2 If so, is it worse in the playground?	☐	☐
classroom?	☐	☐
corridors?	☐	☐
3 Are there enough bins provided?	☐	☐
4 Are they regularly emptied?	☐	☐
5 Do you ever drop litter?	☐	☐
6 If so, what and why?	☐	☐

Pupil details

Sex M ☐   F ☐   Class ☐

Litter survey

	Yes	No
1 Do you ever notice litter in the street?	☐	☐
2 Does it concern you?	☐	☐
3 Are your objections on the grounds of		
hygiene?	☐	☐
tidiness?	☐	☐
4 Are there enough bins provided here?	☐	☐
5 Is rubbish regularly cleared away?	☐	☐
6 Do you live locally?	☐	☐
If so, would you pay more rates to get a better		
service?	☐	☐
7 Do you drop litter?	☐	☐
8 What can be done about litter?		

Interviewee details

Sex   M ☐   F ☐   Age (approx)

less than 20	20–35	35–50	50–65	over 65
☐	☐	☐	☐	☐

Passenger questionnaire

1 Point of departure

2 Destination

3 How often do you travel by bus?
- Daily ☐
- More than once a week ☐
- Less than once a week ☐
- Infrequently ☐

4 What is the purpose of your trip?
- Work ☐
- School ☐
- Shopping ☐
- Other ☐

5 What improvement would you like to see in the service provided? _____

6 Are the buses usually on time? ☐
- late? ☐
- early? ☐
- Don't know ☐

7 Are the buses busy? Do you get a seat?
- Always ☐
- Usually ☐
- Never ☐

Passenger details

Sex M ☐ F ☐ Age (approx)
- less than 20 ☐
- 20–35 ☐
- 35–50 ☐
- 50–65 ☐
- over 65 ☐

Passenger questionnaire

1 Station of departure _____

2 Destination _____

3 How often do you travel by train?

Daily ☐

More than once a week ☐

Less than once a week ☐

Infrequently ☐

4 Do the rail times suit you? _____

5 What is the purpose of you trip?

Work ☐

School ☐

Shopping ☐

Other _____

6 What improvements would you like seen to the service provided? _____

Passenger details

Sex   M   F

Age (approx)

less than 20 ☐

20–35 ☐

35–50 ☐

50–65 ☐

over 65 ☐

A seaweed weather station, see page 74

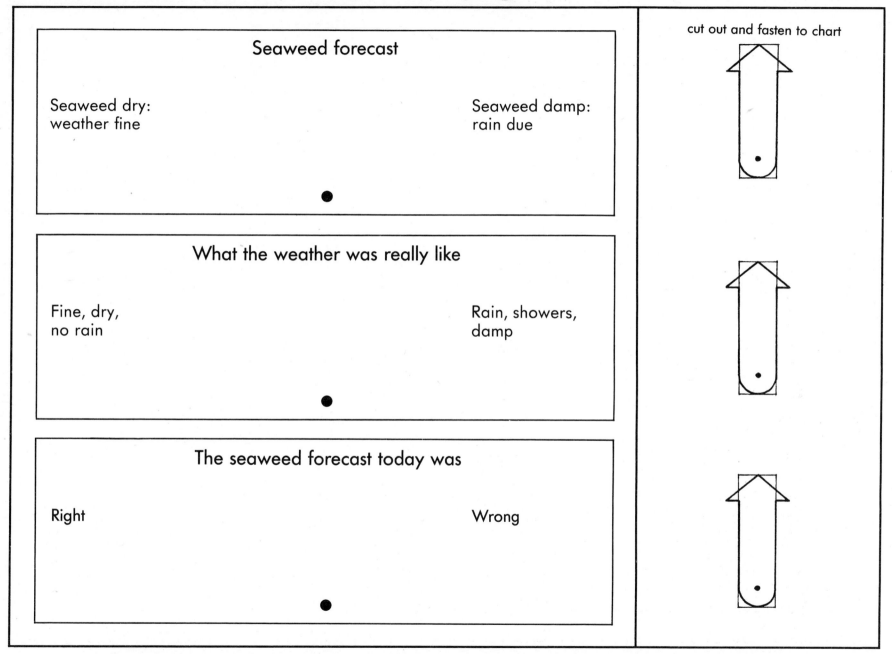

Seaweed forecast

Seaweed dry:
weather fine

Seaweed damp:
rain due

What the weather was really like

Fine, dry,
no rain

Rain, showers,
damp

The seaweed forecast today was

Right

Wrong

cut out and fasten to chart

How high is the tree?, see page 97

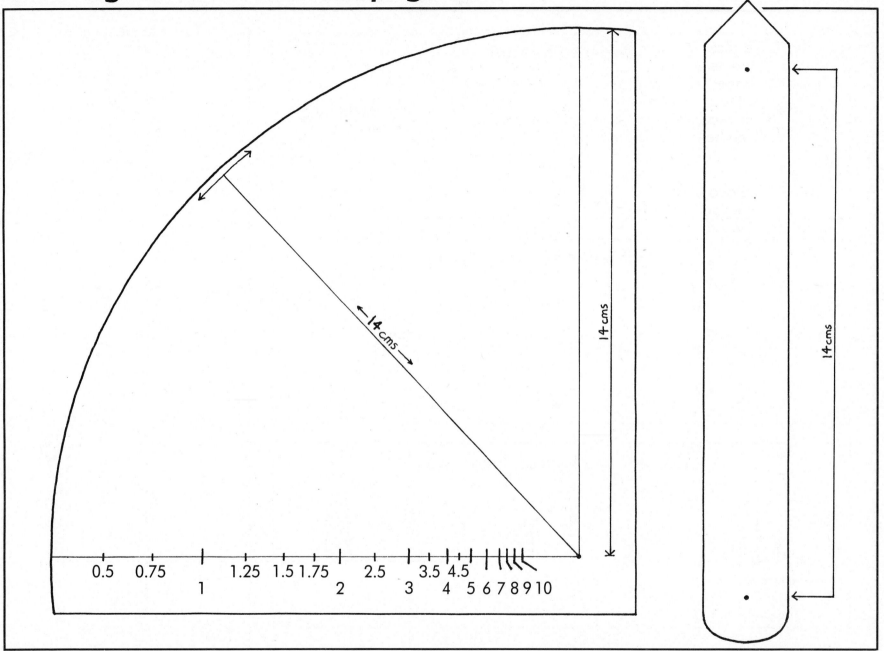

How high is the tree?, see page 97

To use
1 Measure the distance from the base of the tree.
2 Hold the clinometer vertically at eye-level, and point the arrow to the top of the tree.
3 Read where the string crosses the scale.
4 Multiply your reading by the distance measured.
5 This is the tree height (plus your own height).

To make
1 Stick the photocopied sheet on to firm card.
2 Cut the pointer and the scale out.
3 Hang the string from the pointer with a weight, such as a cotton reel.
4 Attach the blunt end of the pointer to the scale card with a paper-fastener.

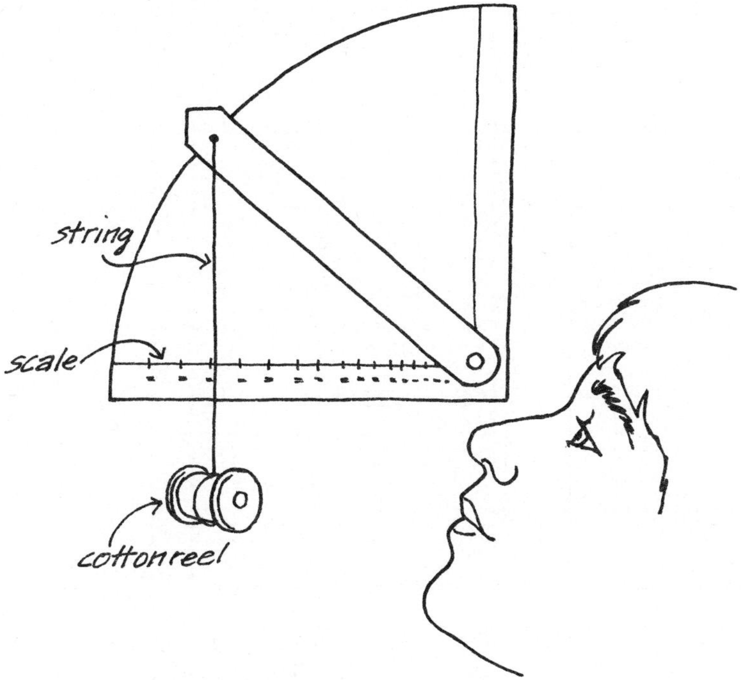

string

scale

cotton reel

height

distance

Measuring the rainfall, see page 103

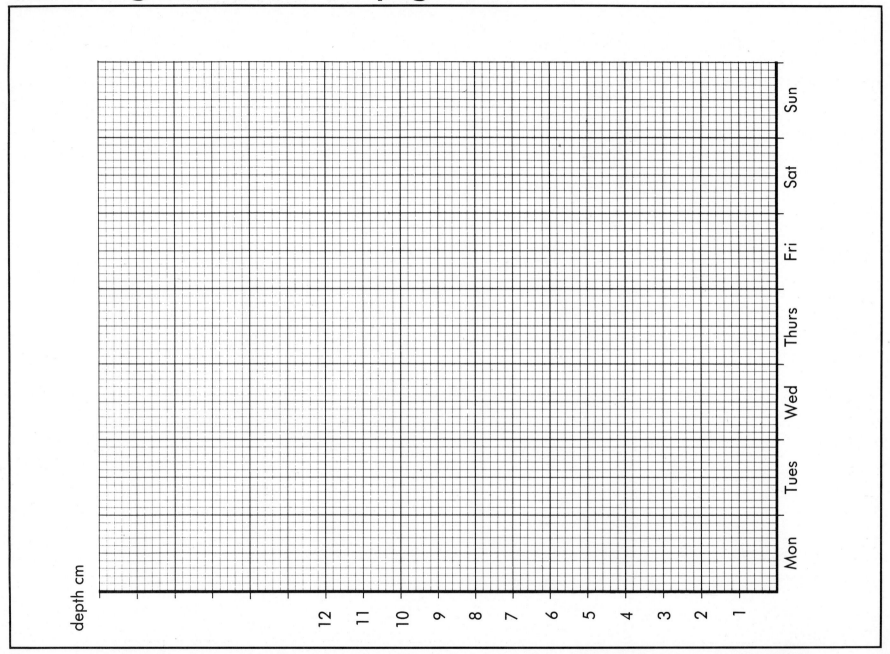

Wind direction, see page 105

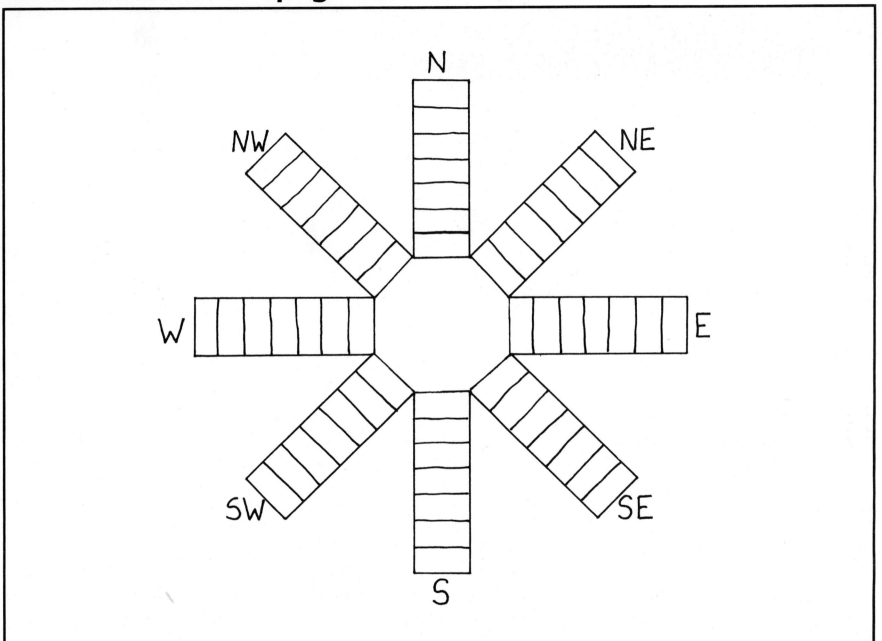

Measuring temperature, see page 108

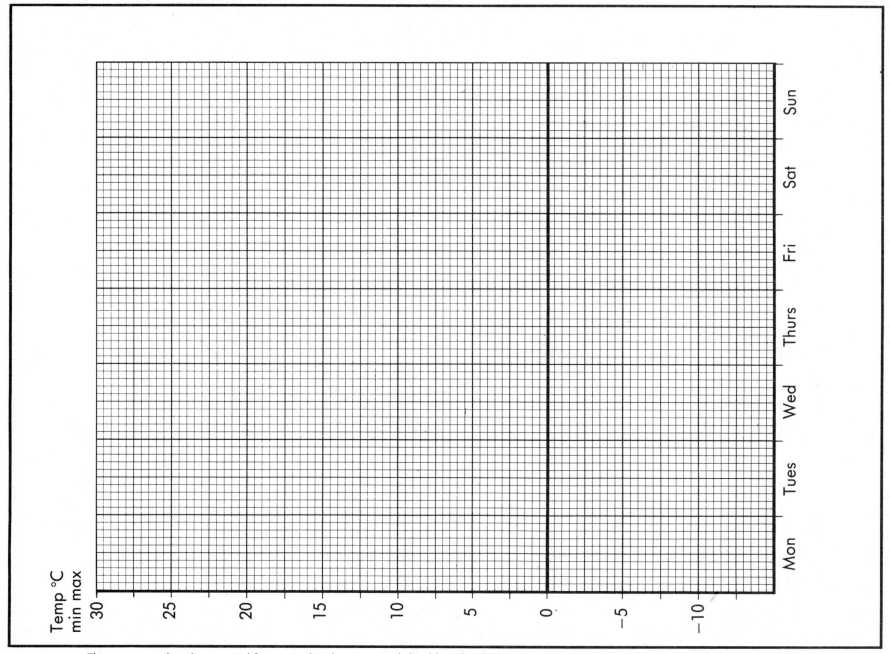

Wind strength, see page 115

Observation	Description	Windspeed (mph)	Beaufort scale
smoke rises straight up	calm	>1	0
smoke drifts, wind vane stationary	light air	1 – 3	1
leaves rustle, vane moves	light breeze	4 – 6	2
leaves move, flag lifts	gentle breeze	7 – 10	3
wind raises dust and paper small branches move	moderate breeze	11 – 16	4
small trees sway, crest on waves	fresh breeze	17 – 21	5
large branches move umbrella hard to use	strong breeze	22 – 27	6
whole trees move, hard to walk against wind	near gale	28 – 33	7
twigs break off, hard to walk	gale	34 – 40	8
chimney pots, slates fall	strong gale	41 – 47	9
trees uprooted, buildings damaged	storm	48 – 55	10
widespread damage	violent storm	56 – 63	11
widespread damage	hurricane	64<	12

Other Scholastic books

Bright Ideas
The *Bright Ideas* books provide a wealth of resources for busy primary school teachers. There are now more than 20 titles published, providing clearly explained and illustrated ideas on topics ranging from *Writing* and *Maths Activities* to *Assemblies* and *Christmas Art and Craft*. Each book contains material which can be photocopied for use in the classroom.

Teacher Handbooks
The *Teacher Handbooks* give an overview of the latest research in primary education, and show how it can be put into practice in the classroom. Covering all the core areas of the curriculum, the *Teacher Handbooks* are indispensable to the new teacher as a source of information and useful to the experienced teacher as a quick reference guide.

Management Books
The *Management Books* are designed to help teachers to organise their time, classroom and teaching more efficiently. The books deal with topical issues, such as *Parents and Schools* and organising and planning *Project Teaching*, and are written by authors with lots of practical advice and experience to share.

Let's Investigate
Let's Investigate is an exciting range of photocopiable maths activity books giving open-ended investigative tasks. The series will complement and extend any existing maths programme. Designed to cover the 6 to 12-year-old range these books are ideal for small group or individual work. Each book presents progressively more difficult concepts and many of the activities can be adapted for use throughout the primary school. Detailed teacher's notes outlining the objectives of each photocopiable sheet and suggesting follow-up activities have been included.